Steve Halliwell was educated at Kirkham Grammar School in the 1950s and early 1960s. A wide range of occupations and periods of self-employment, saw him retire at around 60 years of age.

He now finds himself as busy as he's ever been, researching and writing about a collection of interests, including the local history of his birthplace, an area he has lived for the bulk of his life.

Other Books by the Same Author.

Preston Pubs, Amberley Publishing (2014)

Moses Holden 1777 – 1864, Vanguard (2016)

Moses Holden 1777 – 1864, Canopus Books, (Second Edition - In print), (2021)

The Lancashire Bare-knuckle Fighter and Livery Stable Keeper. Minster Park Publishing, (2021)

Pubs in Preston

Plough to Plau

And Fourteen other INN-side Stories

Stephen R. Halliwell

Minster Park Publishing

A CIP catalogue record for this title is available from the British Library.

Contacts for the author:

29 Minster Park, Cottam, Preston. PR4 0BY

Email: srh.steve@aol.co.uk

Website: https://pubsinpreston.blogspot.co.uk

ISBN 978-1-9196163-1-5

First published in 2021

Printed   by: Inky Little Fingers,

Gloucester.

Dedication

As is my custom, I again dedicate this book to my precious grandchildren, Oscar, and the twins, Phoebe and Eliza, with the simple message that whatever you do with your lives, be creative.

Don't just follow the pack but be your own individual selves. Ask questions, both of yourselves and others, and using your early years of learning the difference between right and wrong, embrace the good and discard the bad.

Acknowledgments

Again, I acknowledge the freedom allowed me by my wife, Rita, to follow my inquisitiveness to a worthwhile conclusion.

I also acknowledge the help given by Jeremy Rowlands, the owner of Plau and other similar businesses in Preston. Jeremy guided me through much of the background history that has only recently come to light, but also, along with his colleague, Nick Elsby, provided me with a lot of photographic material concerning the restoration work.

Danny Taylor, the landlord at the Black Horse Hotel on Friargate, has also been extremely helpful with some of the historic aspects of this relatively young (only 123 years old in 2021) building, and along with David Toase, provided me with many photographic images to accompany my story.

I thank you all.

Chapters

Above: The Plough Inn - As it was bought in 2015.

Local Historian, the late Paul D. Swarbrick (left) and his partner, Gill, both members of the Preston Historical Society, make suggestions and offer encouragement, relative to the building's future.

From the Plough Inn to Plau

Friargate Brow

A choice had to be made as to which story should have the honour of being the flag-bearer to lead the rest of the team, and for several reasons, the Plough Inn, now Plau, standing as it does on the summit of Friargate Brow has most, if not all, the credentials. The principal of those reasons lie at the feet (and as you will later discover, the hands) of the most recent owner of the property, a mere century after it closed its doors as a licensed property in 1913.

The new owner, Jeremy Rowlands, is an entrepreneurial businessman and licensee who Preston is fortunate to have as a resident. He could, quite easily have stripped out all that the eye could see and re-covered the resultant bare walls with commonly available modern décor. An early decision was made however, to dig a little further. It turned out to be forty-three feet further; and what has been discovered could possibly change the content of many history books as well as thoughts about the antiquity of not only the Plough Inn, but the whole area in which it stands as well.

I think it appropriate to deal with the Plough Inn as two separate but connected stories, looking firstly at part of the 19th century life of the inn, but including a few years from the century before. We will then move back in time to discover what existed before, the results of what amounted to an archaeological dig, and searches through many documents in the Lancashire Record Office.

The only confirmed reference I had of the place before 1800 were the figures given in the disclosure of Election Expenses incurred during the election of 1795. The following is a summary of those expenses which were paid by John Watson, an agent to Lord Derby, to John Leach, the landlord at the Plough. The total of £187 has little meaning compared to values today, but in 1795 it would represent the equivalent of over £20,000.

The breakdown details tell us that in respect of four days eating (snacks) for the musicians on the canvas. At 1/6d (7½p) per day, it amounted to £1. 4s 0d (£1.20). Four days dinner for nine musicians at 1s (5p) each, totalled £1.16.0 (£1.80p). Liquor, to accompany the meal for the same nine men, £2. 4s 6d (£2.23p). An interesting £163. 6. 0d (£163.30p) for "Sundry liquor during the Poll, as per book," is one way of saying, 'the amount paid in bribes to encourage you to vote a particular way'. Finally, the record tells us that £2 was expended on the Saturday 'before the taps were stopped'.

An incident that happened in 1857 took on a new perspective when the 20th century discoveries came to light, for in the July of that year, a young farmer from Sowerby near Woodplumpton, called Thomas Catterall, was charged with attempting to commit suicide, which at the time was a criminal offence. The brewer at the Plough, Edward Williams, in his evidence, said that the previous morning, the prisoner had gone to the inn, and called for two glasses of ale, one for himself, and the other for a man who was in his company. After talking for some time, the prisoner had said that he wished "to make himself away," and somebody who was present in the bar, brought him an unloaded old horse pistol. The prisoner, believing it to be loaded, put the muzzle into his mouth, and 'shot himself'.

When laughter in the courtroom had subsided, they were told that Catterall then went in the yard, and attempted to throw himself into an old well, many yards deep, but the witness and others prevented him from doing so. A policeman was sent for, and when he arrived, he found the prisoner sprawled on the flags, and "looking for a cart to take him home". Catterall was asked by the court about his circumstances at home, and he told them that he worked for his father, that he had a wife and four children, and he had been on the 'spree' since Saturday. The magistrate, coincidentally also named

Catterall, said to him that he thought they ought to send him to the House of Correction for three months, but he was interrupted by the prisoner who said, "Eh, but I think aw've hed enough yonder (the police office); aw've never tasted nayther meyt nor drink sin aw went in; aw'm whelly starved!" (More laughter in court). The Bench fined him five shillings.

An article that may also have some bearing on discoveries made in the last few years, and thereby forming a link with history, appeared in the Preston Chronicle in early 1864. It was headed, "Among the spirits," and related to a police case where a young man had been charged with stealing whisky. The evening had begun well, with the man entering the Plough Inn in a completely sober condition, but after paying for and consuming just one glass of ale, he was leaving the house in a completely intoxicated state, but a comment made to the landlord, Thomas Walton, caused him to go into what was described as his barn, where he found whisky running from a keg. He estimated that he had lost about a gallon of the liquor and considered that he had an idea where at least some of it had gone.

Despite having left the inn, the man was quickly found and taken to the police station. At a hearing, the following morning he pleaded guilty to the theft and was sentenced to fourteen days imprisonment with hard labour.

The well will be discussed in detail later in the story, as will the barn with the whisky, although not by that name. The following series of incidents will also be given a new life when we look at the 21st century discoveries.

On Monday 7th April 1868, Inspector Hornby of the Preston police apprehended a man named Kennedy, alias O'Hare, in the Plough Inn on Friargate. He was wanted on a warrant by the excise authorities in Liverpool for being the proprietor of an illicit still in that town, and for which he had been fined £100, and in default of the payment of that fine, to be imprisoned during Her Majesty's pleasure. Later the same evening, and after removing the prisoner to the authorities in Liverpool, Inspector Hornby and two of Her Majesty's Excisemen visited the Plough Inn, Friargate, where the landlord Thomas Crane was seen, and asked whether he had an illegal still in his possession, and he told them he had never seen one.

Left: Is this the latch that enabled the brewhouse to be locked from the inside, something that Inspector Hornby, of the Preston Borough Police was aware of when he made his search of the premises looking for the production of illicit whisky?

Photo: Nick Elsby

They asked him for a light, and a search was made of the house, where they found, in one of the cellars, a quantity of distilled whisky, and in another cellar, a further quantity of the same spirit. In a loft over the brewhouse, they found an illicit still, which appeared as though it had been moved recently. They returned to the first cellar, and after a thorough search found a small, locked door about twenty inches square. They asked for the key, but Crane told them there was not one for that door. The inspector told him that if he did not produce a key, they would break the door down. He replied, "Very well," and broke the door down himself. The police officer entered through the small aperture and saw the bed where the still had formerly lain, together with similar brick and mortar debris to that found in the loft. He also found an earthenware jar, which had apparently been recently upset, but it was not completely empty. It was later found to contain a small quantity of 'low wines' which are, apparently, the first 'runnings' of the still from the 'wash' or the first distillation. These are clearly technical terms of the trade, for the liquid was later declared to be a spirit, a commodity upon which duty was payable. It was later established that the still would fit through the door they had broken down, contradicting a statement to the contrary made by Crane.

They went then into the brewhouse, and examined it and the room above it, the one referred to as the loft, clearly accessible through the small door referred to above, as well as from elsewhere. It was a room that was immediately next to Crane's private accommodation. Crane was asked who was present at the time he came into possession of the still, and he said he did not know that it was a still, and that somebody had left it about two months ago. Unfortunately for him, whilst they were in this upper room, Inspector Hornby's attention was attracted to Mrs. Crane, who was elsewhere on the premises, busily removing a quantity of spirits from the kitchen to a position up the staircase of the house. One of the excisemen took possession of a gallon of what they believed, and later confirmed to be, either smuggled or illicit whisky, with a strength that was 26.6° over-proof, which is a product that was illegal to be distributed by dealers. Crane was asked why his wife was moving the liquor, that was in a corked, stone jar, and he said he did not know she was doing. He asked Mrs. Crane the same question in the presence of her husband, and "got nothing but abuse."

In his evidence to the court, Inspector Hornby said that he had reason to believe that the man Kennedy, alias O'Hare, had led Crane into the affair. He went on to say that three days after their first encounter and search of the premises, he saw Crane again, and on that occasion he admitted he had been a fool in the matter, and that he had let the vault in the cellar to Kennedy, ostensibly for the purpose of making black beer, but that he didn't really know what was going on in the cellar until a short time ago, when he gave Kennedy notice to quit.

Inspector Hornby said that from prior knowledge, he knew that the brewhouse doors were always locked from the inside, and so he had asked Crane that when the still was brought to the house, who had opened the brewhouse door, but he denied any knowledge.

The second part of the story takes us back to a time where details about hotels and taverns are at best scant. Pevsner's Architectural Guides inform us that Preston has a Roman and a medieval past, although none of it remains visible. Snippets from here and there in old legal documents give you the ability to make certain assumptions, but I prefer, wherever possible to keep to the facts. One fact of which we can be certain is that the Plough Inn on Friargate, formed part of the mediaeval and late middle age period of the town of Preston. Back in a time when there were barely more than the three thoroughfares that spread out from the old Town Hall and Market Place area, with Fishergate meeting Church Street, or Church Gate as it was once named, in a continuous line from the River Ribble at the foot of Fishergate Hill, to Stanley Street. The short length of Cheapside, alongside the Market Place, leading directly into Friargate. The three main thoroughfares had little more than linear housing, with, in many cases, lengthy garden areas to the rear, referred to or described as 'burgages'.

It is hoped that you will be able, from the material that several year's meticulous work has uncovered by the new owners, to recognize the link from a time in the 1600s, through the few incidents I have described from the 1800s, from the old well and the cellars and vaults, through to the present day.

Its position on the topmost brow of the hill, means that it was close to an important subsidiary road that runs off Friargate. It was originally called Fryars' Lane, the road which led to the Franciscan Friary of the Grey Friar Monks. It was also a road to the River Ribble, where a ford enabled access to the Penwortham area and beyond to Liverpool. It was later renamed Bridge Street and Bridge Lane, before being altered again to Marsh Lane. The lowest point on the river where there was a bridge was at Walton-le-dale at that time, with the Old Penwortham Bridge being built in 1755, and again in 1759 after the first one collapsed within twelve months.

The Plough stands on the site of a previously unknown building, and although there have been many changes over the years, the principle building that was inherited in 2015, is undoubtedly the same structure that John Chorley built 350 years ago. The property is marked on Kuerden's hand-drawn map of 1684 as being in the possession of Jno. Chorley

The Chorley's were a puritan family in the 17th Century and were much involved in the administration of Preston with several members of the family becoming Aldermen, or Mayor of Preston, including both John Chorley Senior and Junior. Their portraits can be seen in the Harris Museum. By trade the family were variously butchers and haberdashers, and it is thought that the Plough Inn started life as a butcher's shop, as well as providing their accommodation in the 17th Century. Features found in the cellar, such as the stone tables with drainage run off channels, would suggest that it could have been used as an abattoir or meat hanging area.

During the following century, male descendants carrying the family name of John Chorley moved to Liverpool and Jamaica as merchant traders, and unfortunately became embroiled in the slave trade, running the Preston Plantation in Jamaica.

Several inns and taverns were featured during the Jacobite Rebellions of 1715 and 1745, with a part of the first set of skirmishes occurring immediately outside the Plough Inn, which was barely fifteen yards north of where the Old Toll Bar Gate defences were situated. Pictorial representations of the battle show many burning buildings in this part of Friargate, and it is entirely possible that the current Plough Inn building was constructed on the site of one of the buildings either damaged or destroyed in the battle. The original Boar's Head Inn which stood six or seven properties closer to the town centre, and in the keeping of James Wittoll, perhaps suffered the same fate, only to be reborn on the opposite side of Friargate, just a short distance from the Market Place.

Baroness Catherine Petre is the next recorded owner of the building we now regard as the Plough Inn, forming just a part of her extensive estate. She had been born into a well-established Lancashire family of Catholic landed gentry, and was the daughter of Bartholomew Walmesley, who died in 1701. Her brother, Francis, died in 1711 at the age of fifteen years, leaving Catherine, aged thirteen years, as the last of the Walmesleys, and the inheritor of the family wealth. She was considered to be a possible spouse for either Bonnie Prince Charlie, or even James Stuart "the Old Pretender," but on the 1st of March 1712, this much sought-after bride was married to Robert Petre, the 7th Baron Petre, which brought him a £50,000 dowry, and a fifteen-year-old bride. It was a short marriage, for within twelve months or so, Lord Petre had died from smallpox, aged twenty-three, leaving a sixteen-year-old wife, six months into a pregnancy. On his birth, her son, Robert James Petre, succeeded his father as the 8th Baron Petre immediately after his birth.

In 1732, the property was occupied by Thomas Shawe and his wife, but no details exist to indicate whether they were innkeepers, or whether the building was still being used for a different purpose, and for similar reasons it still is not clear when the building may have been converted into an inn.

The Court Leet Records of 1670 tell us that 'Alderman Worden was fined one shilling for a series of misdemeanours he had committed at his Plow Inn', but the position in the town is not mentioned. There is a suggestion that there was an ancient Plow Inn in Churchgate, or Church Street as it is known now, until the early 18th Century, so perhaps it would be wise to disregard that record.

The first written evidence relating to the Plough Inn, Friargate, was in the 1795 Election Record (of bribes, to elect the Earl of Derby), which I have already referred to, and the landlord mentioned coincides with the John Leach we know was present at the time. The fact that £187 was expended at this house alone, may suggest that it was well-established by that year.

The Plough Inn continued to trade throughout the 19th Century and had, as we have already discovered, had a varied and colourful history, and gained a deserved reputation as an unruly house. Part of this reputation came from the attached Dram Shop or Spirit Vault – the curse of both 18th and 19th century life. Around the year 1750, Dram Shops or Spirit Vaults were among the names given to Gin Shops of the day and were a product of the Gin Craze which developed into an epidemic in Georgian Society. Gin had been introduced into Britain in the late 17th Century by the Dutch King of England, William III. The production and sale of gin was completely devoid of regulation, a step taken to stem the import of spirits such as brandy from France. As a policy, it proved to be a disaster, for within a few years seven thousand Gin Shops appeared all over England, with shop owners selling their drink under fancy names like 'Cuckold's Comfort', 'Ladies' Delight,' with 'Knock-me-down', being a mixture of hot spiced ale and punch. Daniel Defoe commented: "the Distillers have found out a way to hit the palate of the Poor, by their new-fashioned compound Waters called Geneva, or Gin, for short. In this context, the 'gin' of the Gin Shop included all grain-based spirits.

A Dram is a measure of Spirit which is the equivalent approximately to a ¼ of a pint of liquor, a little more generous than current measures.

Left: One of Hogarth's famous Gin Lane depictions.

Gin or Dram Shops often started in chemist shops and in many ways were more like shops than inns. They were often located in dismal cellars; hence the term Spirit Vaults, with the term referring to the vaulted-cellar rooms that housed them. There was little in the way of comfort, with no seating, just huge vats of gin waiting to be dispensed to patrons, who were expected to have their drink and leave, or fill up their vessels to consume later. In Hogarth's well-known Gin Lane picture, you can see the cellared steps to the Dram Shop in the bottom left of the picture.

There is documented evidence of the Plough Inn having a Dram Shop, and much of what I am writing in this chapter is a repetition of what is recorded on the history page of Plau's extensive website, www.plau.co.uk. The entrance to it will have almost certainly been separate to that of the inn and is likely to have been situated off Plough Passage an ancient, narrow access road that ran between Friargate and Back Lane (now Market Street West). The "Spirit Vault" was listed again in the sale particulars of 1854 for The Plough Inn. However, with the growing public health concerns and the rise of the temperance movement, the Dram shop was legislated out of business around this time.

Right: Internal signage, exposed during the renovations describe its use from well over 100 years ago.

Left: Only an inch or two of space separated the ceiling of the vaults from the mountain of bricks and rubble that was piled within their walls.

Photos: Nick Elsby

"During our renovations, we discovered The Vaults, filled to the brim with rubble and bricked up. After removing fifty tonnes of rubble, the Spirit Vaults started to come back to life, more than 160 years after their closure," recalled Jeremy. In 2018 The Dram Shop reopened, and a drink can be enjoyed again in this atmospheric and timeless space, albeit with a little more comfort than if you had wandered in from the Plough Passage in the 1820s or earlier. The front part of the cellar has been identified by a specialised historian as containing the remains of a small gin distillery, with the historic fabric, particularly in the cellar, suggesting a strong connection with the 18th Century gin craze, and hinting at a date between 1732 and 1751.

Above: The vaults are now far more distinctive, with the contour of the ceiling suggesting further vaulting close by. Hand-made bricks are stacked for future use despite their minimum 300-year life. **Photo: Nick Elsby**

Is this more reminiscent of Hogarth's Gin Shop drawings?

There was a mash pit for pulping the grain and horse-shoe shaped shelving, with water run offs, which held Gin Stills. Small scale gin production had largely been legislated against during the middle of the 18th Century and the construction would appear to be too permanent to be an illegal Still, with the likelihood that this dates from the "Gin Craze" days of the first part of the 18th Century, when gin production was liberalised to encourage domestic spirit production. Indeed, the mash pit and still stand are key features in the identification of such a Gin Shop.

Left: The exposed roof timbers that have been retained in the front, first floor room, but insulated efficiently from the elements, giving a feeling of openness. This room now functions as a beautiful, wood panelled dining room.
Photo: Nick Elsby

On the first floor of the property were found several historical features. The reed and plaster ceiling in the rear room was completely different to the open ceiling and historic roof timbers in the front room. The open roof timbers have been retained in the renovation, with insulation work to the underside of the roof effected, whilst retaining the original appearance. In the front gable end, and discovered when cladding was removed from the exterior and interior, was a beautiful circular window that had been concealed from a street view. This, too, has been removed, renovated, and replaced, to allow passers-by on Friargate Brow to see it once again.

Left: The roof timbers are still visible in the first-floor dining area, with its large timber replacement bay window that overlooks Friargate.

Photo: Nick Elsby

There is an irony in the fact that this one-time Gin Shop might have played a significant part in the Temperance Movement for which Preston is well known. In the autumn of that year, John

21

Finch, an iron merchant of Liverpool, a member of the Temperance Movement there, and a business partner of Thomas Swindlehurst of Preston, encouraged him to reform from being a heavy drinker to one of moderation. He was astonished to find that Thomas had gone a step further, and adopted total abstinence, having found it impossible to be merely moderate.

Thomas had taken his momentous decision in the Plough Inn, sitting with his fourth drink of the day, he began talking to it! I suspect you know you have reached rock bottom when you start talking to a glass of ale? "Pretty sparkling thing, may I taste thee? Then I am undone forever, for this is my last chance for reform! I will not – cheat, deceive, lie, thieve. Devil thou art, I will not taste thee again for twelve months." He maintained it for the rest of his life, but his partnership with Finch as roller makers was dissolved in 1838.

The commonly accepted date for the Plough Inn's renaming to the Hotel National is around 1900, and, despite the name Plough Inn being applied to it in various court cases as late as 1896, I have seen the original Licensing Court Register which details that the name was changed to Hotel National as early as 1882.

The 1896 case referred to in the last paragraph was typical of many in this insalubrious area of the town, densely populated with principally Irish immigrants who lived in the Canal Street region, an area which has now been largely consumed by the University of Central Lancashire. Their Foster Building is a recognition of Foster Square, on whose footprint it stands, and the recently established university pedestrianised area that were previously two huge traffic roundabouts, was a densely packed conglomeration of cotton-workers' dwellings, a majority of whom were of Irish descent.

An incident at the Plough Inn, just before Christmas 1896 was headed 'An Irish Row,' and involved one Patrick Devine and his better half, and Anthony Kelly, the husband of the landlady. It was alleged that Kelly entered the bar and dragged Devine over a barrier before he knocked him senseless to the floor. He then struck him twice with a ginger beer bottle. Devine prosecuted Kelly for the assault, and when he appeared in court, he had his head covered by a bandage. In his defence, Kelly claimed that Devine had been using foul language towards Mrs. Kelly, and that in trying to throw Devine out of the house, he had stumbled over a barrier and sustained his injuries in the fall. There was a cross-summons against the Devine couple brought by Kelly, in which it was stated that the Devine's had returned in the evening and 'kicked up a shindy'. The Bench unsurprisingly took the view that it was a case of six of one and half-a-dozen of the other and fined all three of them five-shillings each.

Incidents such as this were commonplace in many beer-houses and taverns, and in the early part of the 20th Century many closed their doors for the final time, with many of them described as decrepit, dirty, and lawless. In the period between 1890 and 1925, Friargate alone, including those in alleyways off it, lost more than half of its inns and beer-houses, many with the revocation of their licensees by the magistrates. The Plough Inn succumbed in 1913 when last orders was called for the final time. Others included the neighbouring Crown and Thistle, Roast Beef Tavern, Prince of Wales in Clayton Gate, the Empire Inn that had at one time been known as the New Roast Beef Inn, the Old Sir Simon, the North Lancashire Hotel, and many others in Friargate and beyond. The Plough Inn remained empty throughout World War One and was next opened in 1923 as the short-lived Bell's Restaurant. After this time, the building has had an assortment of uses, including a fish and chip restaurant, a furniture store, a watch maker, an alternative clothing shop and latterly Ozone – a retro-clothing and body piercing combination. In the 1950's the building was bought by the Odd Fellows Society with the upper floor being used as a meeting hall for the Society right up to the 1990's.

After the clearance of the Vaults, and as part of the repairs, the decision was taken to remove what remained of the brick floor and to dig down to help try and make the cellars watertight. Water ingress in this area was presenting the team with a big problem; however, one area of the floor was a particular puzzle. When the rainwater came in, it never created a puddle – it drained away from this point as fast as it came into the cellars.

It was the end of a hard day, but curiosity got the better of us, explained Jeremy, and we decided to have a little dig. About a foot under the brick wall, we started to find one of stone. We continued to dig well into the night and the early hours of the next morning. It became apparent that we had found a stone well. We pulled out lots of pottery, clay pipes and even a domino piece made of bone. Over the coming months, the well was eventually excavated below the water table, to a depth of 43 foot.

The large, stone well is of exceptional build quality for such a structure, being constructed of uniform Ashlar Sandstone blocks for the full depth of the well, which suggests it was built by an individual or an organisation of high status. The well clearly predates the current building which is brick built.

Right: The well has been identified as being almost certainly of medieval origin, built at some point between 1100 and 1600 A.D. As far as Preston is concerned, where there is nothing similar that remains visible from this period, it is a significant discovery. No written references to the well have been found, but bearing in mind the quality of the construction, could the well have been built by the Monks  *of the Grey Friars Friary? The Plough Inn is built adjacent to the Grey Friars estate. Or could it have been a part of the nearby Preston Manor House which was located roughly where the British Telecom building is on Moor Lane today. Perhaps we will never know.* Photo: Nick Elsby

There are foot holes carved into the inner wall to allow the climbing of the well. In the first six feet or so we removed a good deal of pottery, clay pipes, and other items of interest. Several items we found can be dated from their inscriptions and all date back to the 1850s, which we can assume was when the well was infilled. Two reasons might account for this, firstly the incident in 1857 where a customer threatened to throw himself in it, and secondly, it was around this time that Friargate first received running water.

Left: Now sealed off, the old well is preserved and protected by strengthened glass. The workmen demonstrate their confidence in their own handiwork.

Photo: Nick Elsby

Finally, and some 105 years after last orders in 1913, all the history had been stripped away. All the modern fittings have gone, and we had rediscovered the essence of the old Plough Inn, and with the restoration and re-imaging of the space, we now have premises that their owners can be proud of, and where the gin and the beer is once again flowing in this historic Preston drinking hole.

I am now able to add a little more to this ever-evolving story, because at the side and the rear of The Plau, is Plough Yard, an ancient passageway that extends to Back Lane, or Market Street West as it is now known, where there are a number of old weaver's cottages fronting onto Market Street West. They comprise a courtyard that formed part of the property that was purchased in 2015 and are being painstakingly renovated and refurbished to form an additional alternative eatery. At the time of writing, this new development is likely to carry a name that reflects its position on Market Street – 'The Market Street Social'. It will be accessible from Market Street, although the majority of their custom will access it from Clayton's Gate, yet another of the area's named alleyways. In the Friargate of the 1800s, passageways and courtyards such as this one were so full of bustle and life, and it is that sort of ambience that the owners are attempting to recreate.

From The Plough to Plau.

Above: The modern cellar equipment is a far cry from that of 1913.

Photo: Nick Elsby

*Above left: The dangerous, well-worn steps down to the cellar and vaults,
and now (right) present a different feel, with handrails to guide your way.*

*Above: The attention to detail displayed during the renovations is
demonstrated in this photograph, where a replacement piece of material
has been created to effect a repair to a portion of damaged ceiling paper.
All photographs: Nick Elsby*

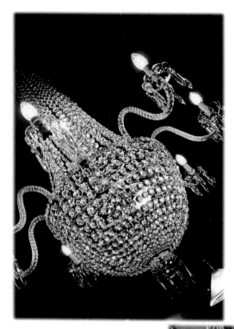

Left: Just one of the five chandeliers that now hang in Plau. In the photograph below you can see the daunting task faced to construct what you see here.

Photo: Nick Elsby

Right: Authentic light fittings were procured at an auction, the basic skeletal frames, and the myriad of integral pieces of crystal, which were painstakingly reconstructed by Jeremy's wife, Rebecca Scott, who is also a

partner in the business, and who was formerly a jewellery designer. She recreated five such light fittings that now hang in Plau.

Photo: Nick Elsby

The hand-made bricks have been revealed and pointed in their entirety. The 19th Century circular leaded window in the gabled roof space has been released from its cocoon and renovated to give it a fresh life. The entrance door to the right is mirrored by the old entrance to Plough Yard that extended as far as Market Street West.

Photo: Stephen R. Halliwell

The Anglers' Inn

Pole Street

The natural corollary to fishing is a 'good honest ale-house,' for in the words of Izaac Walton, "anglers are all such honest, civil, quiet men," and they have need of refreshment after coaxing the elusive fish with patience and meditation.

How many citizens of Preston, necessarily now of a certain age, passed along Pole Street without casting a glance at the Anglers' Inn, a perfect specimen of a Victorian inn, unspoiled to its end it was claimed, by modernity?

The Anglers' Inn, by comparison with many other inns, was not old. It was erected a little before 1840 but had changed imperceptibly by the time of its demise in 1969.

The land on which it was built was formerly a stone-mason's yard, and its most noticeable feature was the large and characteristic sculptured stone plaque over the Pole Street entrance doorway. It depicted an angler in the act of fishing.

He wore the quaint costume of the time, which included a semi-tall hat, his fishing basket was slung over his shoulder, and in his left hand he held the fishing net, as if about to receive the fish he had just caught. In the other hand is the rod, complete with line, held aloft. The whole composition was a delicate and attractive work of art that was, it is believed, carved in marble, and then covered with a form of plaster. It has been recorded that the subject was the first landlord of the Inn, Matthew Brown himself, but much more recently I have discovered that it was  one of his friends, and a man with whom he enjoyed his fishing, called Tom Banks. I received a letter from an elderly lady who told me that when she was a child, her grandfather had told her that the sculpture was of her three times great grandfather, one Thomas Banks, 1781 – 1865, who lived on Bell Street, itself off Pole Street. She was told that he and Matthew Brown regularly went fishing together. Indeed, it was the same Thomas Banks who was the inspiration in the name of the once famous strong ale, Old Tom Ale, despite an 'Old Tom Cat' appearing in the advertisements for the product. Many were the inns and taverns that displayed in their windows the image of a highly coloured face of a cat, with sly, wide open eyes and thick strong whiskers, with the slogan underneath "Try our Old Tom!"

The inn was initially owned by Matthew's brother, Joseph Brown, and the first licence was held by him in 1839, but within months it was transferred to Matthew Brown, and he was to stay for twenty years. I doubt that he was restricted to bar duties for all of that time; he was too interested in creating the brewing empire that he is best remembered for. In 1842 Matthew advertised in the local press, that "he had succeeded in brewing a BITTER ALE, of fine quality, which is much approved from it containing the fine aroma of the hop." He went on to add that even with the limited facilities he had in his brew-house at the Anglers' Inn, he "constantly keeps on hand Ale, Porter, and Table Beer, in hogsheads, barrels, half-barrels, quarter-barrels and six-gallon casks. Table Beer made up to order at the shortest notice." Joseph Brown, however, acquired premises on the diagonally opposite corner, and opened another beerhouse, 'The Britannia,' and began to brew his own beer there, but unfortunately, by 1842, Joseph became an insolvent debtor, and the property of which he was the tenant, was the subject of an auction at the Castle Inn on Market Place in mid-February of that year. Whether it was Matthew Brown who bought the property or not, is not known, but it was on the same corner that Matthew ultimately constructed his large brewery, which was to expand exponentially over the next few years.

After Matthew had left the Anglers' Inn in 1859, he moved to a house on East View facing the Deepdale Recreation Ground, and just before his death in 1883 he moved to Moorfields in Ribbleton, but his affections were always with the inn, and once his company became a limited liability company, the obligatory Annual General Meetings were held at the inn, and shareholders were there entertained to a luncheon. It was the meeting place for many trade societies and other organisations, and it was famous for its catering.

In his later years Matthew Brown was an enthusiastic and highly successful farmer and breeder of cattle. He was a self-made man, and in appearance was said to be a true John Bull type, clean shaven, with neck whiskers and deep-set shrewd eyes, and he farmed several acres at Radholme Laund, Whitewell.

Matthew's successor at the Anglers' Inn was Joseph Tate, who was presented with the opportunity of making his own mark on the place, with the twenty-year recurrence of the famous Preston Guild of 1862. At this particular Guild, the procession of the Smiths, a combination of blacksmiths and silversmiths, began from the Anglers' Inn. They were headed by a man in armour on horseback, a representation of Vulcan, behind which equestrian group came a lorry drawn by two horses. On the lorry was a workman's bench, at which were engaged three men and a boy, making, and fitting up the framework of a lamp for Joseph Tate. Again, when the curtain came down on the Anglers', the same large, and impressive lamp was still hanging, after over one hundred years, above the Lord's Walk entrance to the inn.

Even earlier than the Guild, the new lessee of the inn, in inviting support for himself and his business, began to offer accommodation, with well-aired beds and good stabling. There are no records of Matthew Brown offering either. Again, before the Guild, Tate has engaged himself as a livery stable, and acquired the equipment and carriages to enable him to offer mourning coaches and hearses. It is certain that the first of these offerings would benefit from the huge increase of the visiting population during Guild Week.

Arches are an important and integral part of all Guild festivities but are chiefly restricted to the main thoroughfares of Church Street, Fishergate, and Friargate, plus New Hall Lane and Adelphi Street, so it was a little odd to find a fine one in Pole Street, immediately opposite the Anglers' Inn. Just how influential Mr. Tate and particularly his predecessor had been in the erection of it is not known, but it was described at the time as "most profusely and elaborately decorated with flowers and evergreens. Across the centre of the arch the words 'Independent Order of Oddfellows, M.U. Guild Demonstration.' In the centre, above, and surmounting the arch, was a large and exceptionally beautiful crown, surrounded with flags, evergreens, and so on. Amidst the evergreens, in the centre, were several game birds, which gave the whole a very natural and pleasing appearance. Several parts of the arch were fitted up for illuminations. On the opposite side, in the centre of the arch, is the motto 'Long Live England's Queen.' The arch has a massive and yet cheerful appearance, and when illuminated, its proportions are shown off to great advantage."

As the years passed, Joseph Tate expanded his business interests, from initiating an omnibus service to Blackburn, where a carriage, drawn by four horses and carrying twenty people at two-shillings a head return, compared to the equivalent return journey by train at three-shillings.

He also took possession of some quality thoroughbred stallions, which at appropriate times would tour the whole area, offering their services to thoroughbred mares at five guineas, and all other mares, three guineas. The groom was also a beneficiary from the stallions' services, in the sums of 10 shillings and 5 shillings, respectively. The first of these stallions was 'First Lord,' an animal with a fine pedigree going back several generations, and 'Surat,' a half-brother to 'Kettledrum,' a horse that, in 1861 won the Derby, and came second in both the 2000 Guineas and the St. Leger. There is an interesting local connection to Kettledrum, in that he was bought at Doncaster in 1861 when he was a yearling, for 400guineas, by George Oates the trainer, for his patron, Charles Townley of Townley Hall, Burnley.

Finally, when the inn was demolished in 1969, the fisherman plaque above the main entrance was taken to the company's brewery in Blackburn, and 'put into storage'. Nobody is able or willing to tell you where it is now.

Above: Matthew Brown and the majority of his family are buried in and around this impressive memorial grave in Preston Cemetery.

A 'Bus from the Black-a-Moors Inn

Lancaster Road

From the moment it first opened its doors at the beginning of 1831, it attracted landlords who can only be described as entrepreneurs. Not all were interested in the same line of business, although animals do seem to have been the common denominator. For many years, almost from when it first opened on the first day of 1831, it had a Thursday Cattle Market where all manner of stock exchanged hands, and during the annual Preston Horse Sales in the second week of January each year, these premises were a leading contributor, with full use being made of the extensive stables and yard at the rear. In the mid-1870s there were two sales of a large quantity of fat Icelandic sheep and sixty Icelandic mountain ponies, landed on the quay at the bottom of Fishergate Hill and driven up the incline into Fishergate and Lancaster Road to be sold at the Black-a-Moor's Head Inn. They had been conveyed by steamer directly from Iceland and must have created an interesting spectacle as they were driven up the hill and along the main streets.

Above: The beautiful stained-glass window over the main, Lancaster Road entrance to the Black-a-Moor's Head Hotel, had been in its position for possibly 180 years, until it was decided that it was 'distasteful'. It was replaced by a plain piece of glass. A leading member of Preston's active Black History Society cannot understand what could be distasteful about it.

The land opposite the Black-a-Moor's Head by the time of the above sale of Icelandic produce, included the stop-start Covered Market, begun in about 1870, but delayed by a series of collapses of it during its construction. Prior to the advent of this market, the land occupied by it was known as Chadwick's Orchard, and was an address used by the inn at times during its early existence. On other occasions its address has been given as Lancaster Street, Lancaster Road, Lancaster Road South, and for a reason that is not clear, Ormskirk Road.

For reasons already outlined, entrepreneurial farmers have been attracted to run the inn, giving them the opportunity to further their and others farming activities, some of whom already were, or later adopted the trade of an auctioneer, thus conducting their own sales whilst at the same time filling the inn with hungry and thirsty farmers and other visitors.

A variation to the use of the premises came in around 1857, when George Smith took over the reins, although he had not travelled far to get here. He was to be just one of five successive

Smith family members to hold the licence for this inn. George's father, James, had been the landlord at the neighbouring Golden Cross Hotel, which at that time was enjoying its first incarceration, with an address in The Shambles, and in the early 1850s he took over at the Black-a-Moor's from another of his sons, Thomas. His tenure, however, was not a long one, because at the end of 1856, his wife died, and George shortly afterwards succeeded him.

As Preston continued to grow, and as people began living at further distances from the town centre, the need and demand for transport to those areas grew, and coupled with a growing economy, the need to convey both goods and passengers from one place to another also continued to grow.

The first intimation of George Smith's involvement in the carriage trade was soon after he took over from his father, although it is difficult to imagine that he had not already taken the first steps at an earlier stage. In the early autumn of 1857, an advertisement appeared in the local paper which, among other things, announced that he would continue to supply, on the most moderate terms, hearses, mourning coaches, single and double fly's, and Hansom Safety Cabs 'which are so universally patronised.' The names of 19th century carriages may be a mystery to many, so where possible, I will try and un-fathom it. A 'Fly' was a carriage intended for the carriage of goods rather than people and adapted for such use as circumstances demanded. 'Hansom Safety Cab' was simply the original name applied to the cab designed by York architect, Joseph Hansom, and was a reference to the idea that the carriage was intended to combine speed with safety. They were designed in the mid-1830s, with a low centre of gravity to enable safer cornering. The word 'cab' is a truncation of a word that is still in common usage, 'cabriolet', a reflection of the design of the carriage. In the same advert he was offering for sale a light spring cart, a dual purpose two wheeled vehicle with 'C' springs, used for either the carriage of goods or people depending on the body fitted to the from. Those intended for the carriage of people have acquired the names, governess cart, jaunting cart, or Whitechapel cart. Another alternative name was Tax or Taxed cart, where a tax was payable when carrying specific goods such as wines and spirits.

A couple of years later he advertised that his carriages had been diversified to include a Shillibeer, effectively an omnibus, that had been designed by George Shillibeer. His original designs for his carriage had been on the streets of Paris since 1827, but this fully enclosed form of transport must have been one of the earliest on the streets of Preston. At the same time, he took the opportunity to tell readers that he had a superior stud of twenty horses, to be driven by none but steady and careful drivers. Such a comment was probably necessitated by the adverse publicity he received in 1859, when a man in his employ had conveyed a customer to Salmesbury, but on the return journey had driven the horse so hard, up Brockholes Brow, that on reaching the summit, it fell down dead.

Not content with what had occurred, he then tried to persuade a witness who had seen all that happened, to accompany him to the Black-a-Moors Inn and say that the animal had been driven at a normal, regular, speed, but three other men, who had also witnessed the event, said they would give evidence against him. With that, the driver absconded, leaving his cab and the horse in the road, so one of the men present informed Smith of the circumstances, who shared the information that the man had only been employed by him five days earlier.

Whilst speaking of animals and diversification, it is interesting to note that around this time, George Smith is advertising his nine-month-old well-bred boar that weighed twenty score (about 400lb), and then eighteen months later he has taken a similar advertisement relating to another boar, "King of the West", bred in Cumberland, and previously owned by the landlord of the

Commercial Inn in Lancaster. It was evidently a rather desirable pig, because the serving of a sow at the Black-a-Moor's Head Inn, was to cost its owner 10s 6d each, with payment to be made after the first serving. It is worth mentioning at this point, that his brother, after leaving the premises, had bought a small farm in Broughton, and was no doubt making use of the inn for their mutual benefit.

In 1860, still ten years before the start of any building of the Covered Market, George Smith took over a lease for the whole of Chadwick's Orchard, an area that had hosted innumerable public events and fairs and followed it up by attracting the attention of 'Showmen, and Proprietors of Travelling Theatres', etc., from whom he would be able to draw a rent for its use for their respective purposes.

During much of the 19th century many Burial Societies along with other cooperative groups, provided the resources to pay basic funeral expenses, and George Smith, along with other operators offering funeral hearses and mourning coaches, to keep costs down, were encouraging those in need of their services to approach them direct, rather than go through such societies, who, of course, would like a cut or a commission for their intervention. The co-signatories in an advertisement suggesting direct contact were William Harding, probably the largest carriage operator in Preston, but also Leonard Billington, landlord of the Bull and Royal Hotel, and Roger Bowling, Smith's counterpart at the Red Lion Hotel opposite the Minster in Church Street.

In addition to this protectionism, George is further diversifying his business by offering removals of furniture, using a first-rate spring van which he had just built for that specific purpose, whilst just six months later, he made it known that he had just taken over the livery stables in Mount Street that had hitherto been run by John Hull. Hull had only been in possession of the stables for approaching twelve months, but it gave George the ability to expand his interests, particularly the funeral side of it, overnight.

Nothing ever stood still in the busy life of George Smith, from the constant expansion of his assets, together with the disposal of those goods that had already served their purpose and replaced by younger or newer and better, including his animal stock. An interesting sale of 'that well-known, fast-trotting grey mare, Draffin Meg,' describing her as having finished third of eleven in the Aintree Knowsley Stakes, beating several noted American and Liverpool horses, together with, or separately from a new light sulky, and set of light trotting harness. A sulky is one of those bodyless carriages with just a single seat for the driver, that many will recall the late Duke of Edinburgh racing in.

Accidents to carriages where both passengers and animals are involved tend to have added complications, but one that escaped such, involved an omnibus that had made its regular run from the Black-a-Moors Head to Fulwood, a service that was well patronised. When close to Withy Trees, one of the wheels came off, but was replaced without serious consequences to either passengers or horses. More serious was an incident on Strand Road, where the railway lines cross the carriageway. There's little doubt that the combination of road and rail would be more demanding of care than it is now, but while crossing the rails, the horse's actions or reactions caused the carriage to jerk and swerve to one side, overbalance, causing several passengers to leap from the top of the carriage onto the road. The carriage continued to jerk from one side to the other before it became settled. The passengers inside the carriage were likewise shaken from one side of the carriage to the other, but despite being said to be terrified by their experience, there were no injuries sustained.

A similar episode happened in Lune Street, where a vehicle was being driven from Fishergate towards the Corn Exchange. A group of children playing on a street corner near the Exchange, caused the driver to halt the vehicle so suddenly that the horse fell and broke one of the shafts, but again, no injuries were suffered. Sadly, there were instances such as the occasion when hay dealer John Almond hired a horse and cart to take a load of hay to a farm near Kirkham. On arrival he left the conveyance by the hayrick in the farmyard, but during his absence, several sheaves of straw were blown from an adjacent stack, which alarmed the horse and caused it to back up. Unfortunately, it backed into a pond, cart, load, and horse, and although efforts were made to extricate the horse that Smith valued at £20, by the time it was removed, it was quite dead.

The 27th day of March 1874, saw the demise of George Smith, whose death left his wife to take over the reins at the Black-a-Moor's, and to dispose of all the accoutrements of a livery stable keeper and carriage operator. The answer to her problems were speedily answered by the next landlord, Daniel Ashcroft, a farmer by trade, who not only became landlord of the Black-a-Moor's Head, but is also believed to have bought, in its entirety, the auctioned items. Within a month he was reselling much of what he had purchased, suggesting that we have, in Daniel Ashcroft, another entrepreneur on the premises. The transaction between Mrs. Smith and Ashcroft, was said to have been carried out so cordially that arrangements were made to enable the omnibus service to run on the day of the handover, for the benefit of the new owner. It was not long before Mr. Ashcroft was acting as an auctioneer on his premises, and it was he who sold the Icelandic sheep and ponies mentioned earlier.

It is believed that the Ashcroft's were still owners of the Black-a-Moor's Head when James Trainer became the licensee in 1890 and stayed a couple of years. Trainer was the goalkeeper for the famous Preston North End 'Old Invincibles,' who, in 1888, had won the league without losing a game, and the F.A Cup without conceding a goal. He was a major celebrity in the town, and what a coup to have him behind the bar, allowing the town's football enthusiasts to come and rub shoulders with him. I think that having a celebrity such as Trainer holding the license and managing the house for Daniel Ashcroft, was a shrewd business move. There were several members of the same football team that were used in a similar way. He had only arrived from Bolton Wanderers in 1888, that notable year, and was playing football until the end of the century. It is interesting to note that he came to the attention of Preston North End when they thrashed Bolton Wanderers 10 – nil, and he still managed to impress the Preston manager sufficiently to want him in his team!

The Influence of the Derby Family

The Three Legs of Man forming part of one of the Derby Family Coats of Arms

So much time has elapsed since the Derby family held any sway over the town of Preston, that many people in our communities will have no idea what I am talking about. Their influence as political leaders was immense, with their mansion on the northern side of Church Street, providing evidence of their wealth and influence. The family seat, of course, was Knowsley Hall on the outskirts of Liverpool, but Patten House, formerly the home of Thomas Patten, was later the Preston seat of the Derby family.

If I were to mention just a few words connected to the Derby family, it may give some understanding about the inns and taverns into which I am going to give you an insight. Even younger readers may be aware of the Lord Derby statue in Miller Park, where he stands aloft, surveying the Park as it falls away from him towards the majestic River Ribble. His full name was Edward Geoffrey Smith-Stanley, and he was three times Prime Minister during the 1800s.

Above: The magnificent Preston home of the Derby family until well into the 1800s. It was on the north side of Church Street in the vicinity of Derby Street.

From around 1820, and for a lengthy period thereafter, the Radical Liberals were a political force to be reckoned with, led by Henry 'The Orator' Hunt, and once defeated by them, they began to retreat from the town, and to a great extent, removed their authority over it by doing so. Their influence extended to the Town Council and the main tradesmen in the town. It was said that everything that they did or said was beyond criticism. However, the development of the cotton industry and the progress of radical ideas amongst the working men of the town, changed all that.

It was thought at the time that the town would struggle without their presence, but in many ways Preston never looked back. Joseph Livesey, the Temperance advocate, perhaps unsurprisingly getting another mention in a book about public houses, said at the time, "When the Derby family took offence and left Preston, it was thought by many that its sun had set forever; but we have survived and almost forgotten the shock then felt; and I presume we have learned this useful lesson – that self-reliance is far better than dependence on patronage and favour."

There is one further thing I would like to mention, and that is that the Derby family were the Lords of Man, and of course, the symbol of the Isle of Man are the three legs of Man. We are now able to better appreciate how the naming of our inns took account of the family's presence and importance, remaining as a reminder of that presence for up to a century, and in many cases, longer.

We will begin with the Derby Arms, a name that has been applied to three separate premises. The original one stood on Back Lane, now Market Street, opposite the end of Lord Street when that thoroughfare ran from its current position, through the Town Hall building and the old Post Office building that is being converted into a hotel. The Derby Arms had had a previous life when it was known as the Cock and Bottle and had an association with a cock-fighting pit in Starch House Square close by, but from 1807, which is my earliest record of that name being applied until 1894, it was known as the Derby Arms Hotel. Its end arrived along with many other changes under one of the Preston Town Improvements Acts, but the name lived on by renaming the Joiners' Arms, believed to be owned by the Derby family, higher up Lord Street. The name survived until the arrival of the new Guild Hall building, which began in the late 1960s. 1864 saw the appearance of the other house to adopt the name, the Derby Inn on Ribbleton Lane on the eastern corner of Geoffrey Street. I wonder if the street took its name from Edward *Geoffrey* Smith Stanley, a street that remains to this day?

Probably the best-known Derby inn was the Eagle and Child Hotel, next to the Bull and Royal Hotel in Church Street. It stood where the entrance to Stoneygate is today,

to the west of, and in the shadow of the Minster. It has been known colloquially as the "Brid[1] and Baby," and the "Bird and Banting". I have also found it referred to as "The Church Gates" for seven years during the 1830s. At one time it had a large pictorial sign on the front of the building showing an eagle's nest, with a baby in the nest. There is a legend that suggests that the baby is a representation of the illegitimate son of Sir Thomas Lathom, an ancestor of the house of Derby and Stanley.

An alternative story regarding the origin of the name, tells us that the wife of Robert Fitz Henry, Lord of Lathom, and founder of Burscough Priory, is believed to have been the daughter of Orme Fitz Ailward. 'Ail' means eagle, and 'ward' is another word for 'guard, keeper or protector,' bold, strong, and vigilant as an eagle, thereby demonstrating in the name, the protection of a child. I have also a record of this inn when it was known briefly as Lathom House.

At the neighbouring Bull and Royal Hotel, many a night has been danced away in the beautiful Derby Room ballroom, many of which in years past, were hosted by the political family that gave it its name.

[1] **This is not a spelling error, but a corruption of the word 'bird'.**

The 'Legs of Man' was a name borne by two hostelries in Fishergate. The New Legs of Man formed a close trio of public houses, standing where the Lancashire Evening Post had their offices and printing works. They had been purchased in 1872 by the Preston Guardian newspaper, before later evolving into the more recent paper. The building constructed by the Guardian had a stone medallion of Caxton's head in the centre of the structure close to the roof, and the road where the Lancashire Evening Post moved to in Fulwood was called Caxton Way, thus continuing a connection to the illustrious 15th century printer, William Caxton.

The details that I have for the Old Legs of Man, date from 1796, whereas those for the New Legs of Man begin somewhat later in 1817, but the other two members of the trio that stood almost contiguous one to the other, the Borough Tavern had previously been known as the Holy Lamb, thus seeing the continuance of a lamb on its sign-board, and the Grey Horse and Seven Stars, which had previously been known without its astral appendages, and prior to that, as the White Horse, although the original White Horse lay almost opposite. It is confusing, isn't it? The Grey Horse and Seven Stars stood closest to the old Town Hall at 124, Fishergate, the Borough Tavern in the centre at number 123a, and the New Legs of Man a couple of doors further at number 121.

The Old Legs of Man, was certainly open in 1796, when an election Expenses debt of £550 was incurred. It stood directly across the road from the Old Town Hall, the replacement for which was opened in 1867 and destroyed by fire in 1947, but the inn had disappeared long before that in 1910. It was in possession of the bank on the corner of Main Sprit Weind until they sold it to close neighbours, E. H. Booth, the family grocers, who consumed the building and incorporated into an extended Fishergate frontage. I have spoken to people who, in their youth, could recall the bright blue painted three legs on the front of the building, and the gilded spurs on each of the three heels.

Left: The Old Legs of Man at 3, Fishergate. Notice the recognisable windows of Waterstone's bookshop to the right of the picture. At the time of closure, it was the home of E. H. Booths, the family grocers.

In 1821, the landlord here was Joseph Croft, who was noted as a pioneer of bathchairs in Preston. This mode of transport became fashionable, not only with ladies, but gentlemen as well, and was the successor of the elegant and exclusive sedan chair. They were the invention of James Heath in the City of Bath, hence the name. The occupants inside the carriage, instead of being carried by two men, were now transported in a carriage on two wheels by a single individual. Croft had special business cards printed, the contents of which read: "The carriage may be had at a moment's notice by applying at the Legs of Man, opposite the Town Hall, on the following terms. One person conveyed to any part of the town within the Borough 1/-, and back again before midnight, 6d, or 1/- after midnight. Two persons the same distance, 2/-, and back again 1/- before midnight, or 2/- after. If engaged by the hour, 2/- per hour."

There was also a Legs of Man to be found in Gin Bow Entry, the curious passage from the north-west corner of the Market Place, through to Lancaster Road, or the Shambles as it was then known. It was in the family of William, Mary, and Peter Worden, from 1812 until 1821. Whether it was a simple husband, wife, son continuation I have no idea, but between 1825 and 1829 it was still in the hands of Peter Worden but described in a Street Directory as 'The Board.'

There is a suggestion that the premises are synonymous with the Ram's Head Inn, for in 1812, William Worden has been recorded as the landlord, and there is a convenient gap in my knowledge between that year and 1838 regarding who may have been the landlord.

Many years ago, if we were to have walked from the Old Legs of Man, along Church Street to where Lancaster Road now begins, we would have found but a narrow entrance into The Shambles, a proliferation of butcher's retail outlets from which it took its name. One of the buildings causing the obstruction for all except foot passengers, was the original Stanley Arms. The eastern wall of the public house formed part of the passageway, and the property was demolished in October 1852, to be replaced by the property we now know by a similar name, the Stanley Arms Hotel in Lancaster Road. However, that was not what it was called when it was first built; they wanted to introduce a bit of what was referred to as modernity. They called it the Knowsley Hotel, still retaining a

Derby connection to its name. J. H. Spencer, a reporter with the Preston Herald, writing in the 1940s said, while writing about this establishment, "In the beginning, houses for liquid refreshment were designated taverns, then inns, afterwards blossoming into hotels, but now this latest name suggests the cosiness of a suburban villa." It is quite an irony that the name 'Stanley Arms Hotel' remains high above street level in relief stone work.

Returning to the eagle connection, in Lune Street there was a splendid building known as the Spread Eagle Hotel. There were Spread Eagles as well as Eagle and Childs all over the old Lancashire area. I well recall the magnificent stone, mock pillar, doorway, complete with a panelled oak door, containing the most magnificent leaded lights I can recall outside of a church. They were intricate in the extreme, and yet I cannot recall what they portrayed. I just know they impressed me, as I am sure they did with the hundreds of visiting farmers who would use the hotel when attending the regular markets immediately across the road at the Corn Exchange. What I do not recall was what was described as a conspicuously massive gilt eagle with wings outspread, which was in the centre of the front of the building. It is not known who was responsible for such advertising expertise, but in 1869 the landlord was an Italian-born man called John Della-bella. His father, a man of the same name, and he, had arrived in Preston and set up business in Lune Street, describing themselves as 'Carvers and Gilders.' I further know that younger John aspired to be an artist, and an example of his work was described by an observer as 'crude and massive'. I prefer to imagine that like many Italians, there can be a tendency towards Mediterranean flamboyance, and I therefore choose to presume that it was John Della-bella, either singly or in tandem with his father who were the creators of the sign.

During the 1800s beer houses were able to open their doors at five o'clock in the morning to provide refreshment to market visitors, whereas hotels were more restricted. However, on the corner of Fleet Street and Lune Street, opposite to the Corn Exchange, there was a beerhouse called the Market Tavern. A mystery that I had pondered for many years was probably answered when I discovered an auction sale poster, describing that in 1877 when the Spread Eagle Hotel was offered for sale. The poster read that the items for sale were the 'Spread Eagle Hotel and Market Tavern,' and what I believe to be the case was that the two places were in common ownership, run by

51

individual landlords, but able to take advantage of the law relating to the early opening of beer houses when there was a market adjacent.

Reminders of the Derby family's presence in the town, now city, are all around us, and can be recognized particularly in the names of streets. Derby Street was adjacent to their Preston home, Patten House, and at the rear of that house was Lord Street. Stanley Street is a busy thoroughfare, with Edward Street off Friargate, less so. Knowsley Street in Avenham may well be a nod to the Derby family, but whether Patten Street off Walker Street is a recognition of the house or of Thomas Patten himself may remain a mystery. There must be several other positive examples to be found, together with an equal number where there may still be doubts.

The Butler Street Dozen

The relative tranquillity of the area now occupied by the railway and its attendant station was shattered in 1837, with the arrival of the North Union Railway Company, who built what was to become a major part of the West Coast Mainline railway. A glance at any map of the area immediately demonstrates how Preston is the centre of so many hubs, to destinations in all directions of the compass, and not only by rail.

Imagine the totally new and distinctive cacophony of sound made by the porters employed on the station, and the metallic sounds produced by wheel on rail, that all small boys must have mimicked since that time. The soot emitted during the production of the steam, and the hiss of the steam itself. Perhaps in the early days it was all at a more sedate tempo than it was when I was a lad, and more in keeping with the timpani of clipping and the clopping of the horse-drawn carriages with which they were to compete.

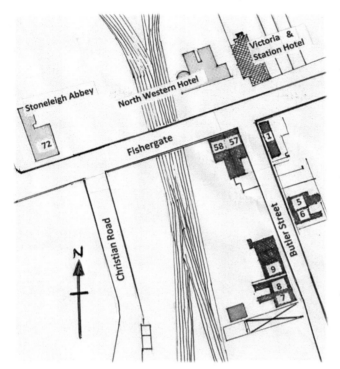

Key to map:

1 Queen's Hotel.
5/6 Railway Hotel.
7 Stevenson Arms.
8 Commercial Inn.
9 Station Tavern

The East Lancashire Hotel,

and

The Bush Inn were north of number 9, but it is not certain where they were positioned.

57/58 North Union Railway Hotel

Imagine the additional sound and characteristic aroma as steam exploded from each side of the newly constructed bridge on Fishergate, below which this new form of transport was to travel to distant destinations, from north and south and from east and west.

The fact that there was a railway in Preston, is said to account for why the town's football team, Preston North End, acquired so many Scottish players. It was largely because Preston was the first major conurbation in England from the north. During the early part of my life, the football club continued to have a close tradition and association with Scottish players, although that no longer is the case.

The introduction of the railway opened up all manner of opportunities for Preston, and the catering trade was one such beneficiary, and while my records may not be entirely complete, it seems that the first hotel that appeared at the same time as the railway, was, unsurprisingly, the 'North Union Hotel,' sometimes known as the 'North Union and Railway Hotel.' It stood on Fishergate, at the corner of Butler Street, on land that is now occupied by part of the railway bridge. It was opened and owned by the North Union Railway Company.

It combined an existing building, the 'Railway Hotel,' and the neighbouring private house, and adapted them for the required purpose. Among many other things it became the home of the 'Railway Guards' Universal Friendly Society,' and was demolished in 1876 / 1877.

The 'Victoria and Railway Hotel' on the opposite side of Fishergate, and facing down Butler Street, was hot on the heels of the North Union, in 1838. This large hotel was to play a major role in the provision of catering services for the better part of two centuries, and although now little more than a bar, it continues in a similar vein.

Of the twelve subjects in this chapter, only the Victoria on Fishergate, and the Railway Hotel remain, but the latter is a later version operating under the name Station Hotel, and on the opposite, or eastern side of Butler Street. This one was only built in 1877, to replace the North Union and Railway Hotel on the Fishergate corner, which had been demolished a year or so earlier to enable widening of the railway bridge.

In 1856, the Queen's Hotel was built on the opposite corner of Butler Street to the North Union Hotel, and for a while, the two stood as sentinels at the head of Butler Street, in an increasingly energised area of the town. They also stood guard over a number of new inns that were springing up on the west side of Butler Street in the early 1850s, to take advantage of the trade attracted by the railway and the station. Closest to the station entrance in Butler Street was the 'Stevenson Arms,' followed by the 'Commercial Inn,' the 'Station Tavern,' and the 'Bush Inn.' The 'East Lancashire Hotel' appeared some six years later, positioned between the Station Tavern and the Bush Inn.

Left: To railwaymen, the Queen's Hotel (later rebuilt as an Insurance Brokers) was known as the 'Top House', to distinguish it from the Railway Hotel, known as the 'Bottom House'. They stood barely 30 metres apart. The Railway Hotel now trades as the Station Inn.

On our arrival back at the head of Butler Street, we would have been able to see the Stoneleigh Abbey on the opposite side of Fishergate, beyond the railway bridge, and roughly where the County Offices now stand. There is no doubt that its owners will have endeavoured to take advantage of the trade available, but in 1877, having already changed its name to the North Western Hotel, the licence for it was transferred to the neighbouring property on the opposite side of the railway lines, a property that had been the home of John Bairstow, the mill-owning philanthropist who created Bairstow Chapel, off Winckley Square, and who was instrumental in the final realisation of the magnificent Harris Institute opposite Avenham Colonnade, when it was known, in 1850, as the Institute for the Diffusion of Knowledge, the forerunner of the University of Central Lancashire. Bairstow Street runs alongside that building.

Right: The North Western Hotel can be seen beyond Harding's Livery Stables, before moving to the opposite side of the railway lines. The pattern on the bridge panelling will be familiar to many.

There is still no sign of the County Offices, beyond.

Following further development between 1897 and 1898, the hotel closed its doors, and an existing inn at the corner of Lancaster Road and Walker Street adopted its name, at the same time relinquishing its former sign of Boilermakers' Arms.

An earlier bridge-widening scheme saw the demise of every single licensed, and other property on the west or railway side of Butler Street. Six properties in total. It is ironic to think that at a time when trade must have been increasing by the week, they were to disappear overnight, but for those left there was hopefully a commensurate increase in their trade.

The bridge extension work involved the introduction of a new thoroughfare down to what is now the main entrance to the station, officially, Broad Street, but more commonly referred to as the station approach. It is now little more than a taxi rank.

Before looking more closely at some of the Butler Street houses, it would be remiss not to mention the 'Park Hotel,' a property that used to be the home of gold-thread mogul, Stephen Simpson. Simpson's works were in neighbouring Chaddock Street and Great Avenham Street. On the face of things, it appears to be set apart from the complex of inns and taverns in the vicinity, but paradoxically, the hotel which was acquired by the London and North Western Railway Company in 1883, is linked by a closed passageway with the station, allowing direct access. It boasted nearly eighty bedrooms, and although it was originally named the 'New Railway Hotel,' it was later renamed the 'Park Hotel,' taking account of its dominant position overlooking the magnificent Miller Park, the beautiful River Ribble, and the floodplain beyond. It is also said, that in addition to the covered walkway for residents of the hotel, there was also an underground passage for the use of staff, to move luggage and other commodities from the station, unobserved.

When we take a closer look at some of the aforementioned taverns, I think we shall have to assume that the Stevenson Arms, a beer-house, took its name from the first licensee, George Stevenson. Serendipity was certainly at play with a name like that, and I wonder if he considered calling his beer-house 'The Rocket'? It is the property shaded green (No. 7) on the above plan, for in a sale notice of 1851 there is mention of the building at the rear that was formerly used as a school, being included in the sale. It can be seen on the plan marked in red.

The school was a private one that was run by Joseph Kenyon, who lived in Butler Street at the time of the 1841 Census. At some point between then and the next Census in 1851, by which time he would have been sixty years of age, he and his family had moved to St. Ignatius' Square in the town.

The Stevenson Arms stood at number seven, so the Commercial Inn at number eight, and the Station Tavern at number nine are simple to place, with numbers running consecutively rather than alternately.

An interesting snippet I found in a legal document relating to the Commercial Inn, was that one of the land and property owners in the street was one John Francis Butler of Pleasington Priory, either the man remembered by the present name of the street, or Richard Butler, his father, who was formerly of Preston.

The Commercial Inn can boast that Rear Admiral, Sir John Ross, the Arctic explorer, stayed at these premises for one night, on his way back to Scotland in 1852. This gentleman may not have had a street named after him, but in his case, an Arctic seabird, a small gull, that is an occasional visitor to our shores. A Ross's Gull is capable of causing a major commotion among the bird watching community, eager to catch even a fleeting glimpse of one.

The only notable occurrences at the Station Tavern would seem to be of tragedies, for in 1855, a lady who was crossing from one side of the railway lines to the other, was struck by an engine and terribly mutilated. She was taken to this tavern, where she was attended by a Catholic Priest, to whom she gave instructions regarding her soon-to-become three orphaned children.

A similar tragedy awaited the young man who fell from the uppermost rungs of a ladder leant against the wall, whilst he was painting the sign of the North Union Hotel in 1866, and was cared for by Alice Walker, the 32-year-old landlady of the Station Tavern. He was particularly unfortunate, for it was a team of horses, in turning into Butler Street with their cart load of coal, that had caught the ladder a glancing blow, with gravity doing the rest! The sixteen-year-old youth involved fell 'with great force' on his head and taken to the tavern. He was attended by a doctor, and the article in the Preston Chronicle concluded that 'Dilworth is progressing as favourably as can be expected under the circumstances.' The opposition paper, the Preston Herald, ended its coverage with the comment 'he now lies in a dangerous condition,' whilst Soulby's

Ulverston Advertiser concluded their piece with 'yesterday Dilworth rallied a little, but it is said that there are no hopes of his recovery.'

This book is not intended to be a chronicle of family histories, but I am sure that there will be readers who will be delighted to discover that in the 1871 Census, Thomas Henry Dilworth, now aged 21 years, is living with his new wife in Peel Hall Street, Preston, and is still occupied as a painter and decorator. In 1881, he is still a painter, now residing in Saul Street, a couple of doors from the Port Admiral Hotel, and can now boast three young sons. Despite the pessimistic predictions, he clearly recovered.

My earliest record for the 'East Lancashire Hotel and Commercial Inn' is in 1857, but its rather confusing name had nothing to do with the above-mentioned Commercial Inn that preceded it by at least six years, but whether it was opened by the East Lancashire Railway Company is likely, but not known. What is known, however, is that in 1865 it was acquired by local auctioneer John Snape, who raised the profile of it by holding several auction sales on the premises. He remained there until his death in 1872, after which his wife continued to run it.

The word 'commercial' would seem to have been appended to a name if there was accommodation available, particularly for travelling tradesmen, salesmen, or company representatives, and such was the case with the 'Bush Inn and Commercial Hotel,' as they were offering 'dinners, soups, and well-aired beds,' thereby offering serious competition to all its neighbours.

In 1862, and in preparation for the Preston Guild of that year, Mark Porter, proprietor of the North Union and Railway Hotel on the corner with Fishergate, advertised that he had added and enlarged, and rebuilt, 'regardless of expense,' entirely new premises, on a 'novel and improved principle,' and expressly adapted for a wine and spirit store, and as a spacious concert hall.' He told his readers that he had engaged the services of first-class artistes from the principal concert halls in England and the Continent.

The concert hall was certainly active for a period of three years, but when Porter left the hotel in about 1865, his successor either had not the same interest in such entertainment, or competition from similar venues had made further progress difficult. In the sale notice when he left, Porter offered the hotel and concert hall for sale, along with the wholesale wine business, which he described as being capable of being run as a separate business.

Whilst we are on Fishergate, let us just pop across the road to the Victoria and Station Hotel, where, in 1869, a Prima Donna of the Italian Opera, Covent Garden, by the name of Mademoiselle Christine Nillson was staying whilst appearing at the Theatre Royal, barely 150 metres away along Fishergate. A telegram from Mr. Gawith, a chemist in Liverpool, dated the 20th of September of that year, and sent to Doughty's of London, throat and lozenge manufacturers, and read, 'Forward by first passenger train, to Mdlle. Christine Nillson, Victoria Hotel, Preston, TWO largest boxes (11 shillings each). Voice Lozenges. Charge to me.'

Left: The Park Hotel. A fine view can be had from the hotel, of Miller Park, and River Ribble beyond.

In a move that is as far away from opera singing as is possible, we will now return to the Park Hotel. In the first few years of the 20th century, the Preston Grasshoppers Rugby Club held an annual dinner in conjunction with their A.G.M. In those days, the club played their rugby on the banks of the River Ribble, and therefore it was an appropriate choice to make for such purposes.

MENU.

SOUP:
Potage de Club Coloree (within a shade or two).

FISH:
Fillet de Sole des ballon bottes anciennes.

ENTRÉE:
Croquette de Referee sifflant.

JOINT:
Braised Fillet of Beef.
French Beans (the only genuine bit of French in the lot).
Pommes de terre nouveau des cigales.

ROAST:
Duckling, or Little Duck (specially pinched from Avenham Park).
Salad   do.   do.

SWEETS:
Apple Meringues.   Kummel Ice.

DESSERT

CAFÉ
(not in the every-day sense of the word).

The menu, particularly in 1903, was full of humorous comment, for instance, next to Soup of the Day, it read, 'Potage de Club Colure,' adding, 'within a shade or two.' The menu continued with 'Fillet de Sole des ballot bottes anciennes,' and 'Croquet de Referee sifflant.' My own translation of the former is 'filleted soles of old football boots,' and the latter, croquet potatoes in the shape or form of a referee's whistle. When it came to announcing that the vegetable accompanying the main course were French Beans, it added that this was the only genuine French item among the whole lot!

Pommes de terre nouveau des cigales is a reference to the club itself. Des cigales is met with in Aesop's fable, and Jean de la Fontaine's poem 'La Cigale et la Fourmi,' 'The Grasshopper and the Ant,' a rather clever connection to the event itself.

It further explained that the Duckling or Little Duck, had been 'pinched from Avenham Park,' as also was the salad that was served with it!

The Port Admiral Hotel

Lancaster Road

The story of Mr. Bond.

For those who remember it, the Port Admiral Hotel was a memorable building, particularly for its grandness and imposing presence. The statues and other magnificent workings in stone were memorable in their own right.

Above: The splendid structure that was the Port Admiral Hotel. The first motion picture in Preston was allegedly shown here in about 1898.

The hotel stood at the corner of Saul Street, on the eastern flank of Lancaster Road, and almost opposite the equally memorable Saul Street public baths. If the saloon bar of the hotel were superimposed on a modern map, you might well be occupying the same global position as the dock of courtroom number three in the new Crown Court building, which along with the city's ring-road, divides Lancaster Road into two separate entities.

One of the more frequent questions I have been asked is whether the Port Admiral had any connection to the sea, particularly as it is so far from where our port was. The answer to the question is, yes, there is, but it is a somewhat circuitous journey to get there. However, such journeys rarely fail to include points of interest and intrigue along the way, and this one is an excellent example of such.

The whole story revolves around a man called Bond. No, not that one, but a native of Blackburn by the name of William. He was born there around 1806, but at about the age of thirty, he moved to Preston. I first became aware of him in the Census of 1841, when I found him to be a beer-seller and contractor, at the Dr Syntax public house in Fylde Road. Along with William and his wife, were two lodgers who were described as stonemasons. It transpired that Bond was a contractor in stone, and a Master Stonemason as well. I am sure you are likely to find him to be a man who is going to make an impression on you, some favourable, others less so.

At that time, the details regarding stonemasonry, did not convey anything other than the fact, but increased in significance later. In about 2005 I received a letter from an elderly lady, Elizabeth Cook, who told me the story that her grandfather, a man called William Bradshaw, who was said to live in Aqueduct Street, and telling me also that it was he who had carved the three statues on the roof of the Port Admiral, in his yard, which she understood to be his backyard. Bearing in mind that these were recollections from when she was a child, I am sure she can be forgiven for imagining it to be in his own yard, particularly if you are not aware that William Bond had a stone-mason's yard in Aqueduct Street. It was there that the work was accomplished. I can add that Bradshaw lived for many years in Byrom Street, a neighbouring street that ran parallel to Aqueduct Street, and if he has conveyed the thought that it was a yard in Aqueduct Street where he did the work, it gives credence to my own thoughts, and Elizabeth's memory.

During the 1840s, William Bond dissolved a partnership he had with another man, concerned with the contracting and carting of stone, but by now he had established his yard in Aqueduct Street. He continued carting on his own account, but as the decade wore on, he began to take an interest in the carrying of freight by sea. Hitherto, his only connection with the river had been an involvement as a yachtsman in a regatta, the Preston Regatta being a regular event centred on the river at the foot of Fishergate Hill, and close to the public house that took its name from the event, the Regatta Inn. In the Regatta of Guild Week in 1842, Bond, in his distinctive orange and blue colours, sailed his boat 'Lady of the Ribble.'

Around the middle of the 1840s a number of disconnected things took place, with the only common denominator being Bond himself. By 1846 he had bought a property in Ashton, close to the Old Quay. It is difficult to establish exactly where it might have been, but in a letter to the Preston Chronicle in October 1846, writer 'Z' complained about the fact that William Bond has stopped up an ancient footpath. The complainant told us that the path ran from the top of the hill near the Old Quay, diagonally behind the residence of Miss Pilkington, to an occupation Road opposite the late James Pedder's. The latter lived at Ashton Lodge on what is now Ashton Park, and it is thought that Miss Pilkington lived opposite on what is now Pedder's Lane. There was also mention that the blocking of the footpath was of considerable inconvenience to parishioners wishing to attend Ashton Church, better known as St. Andrew's, which had opened ten years earlier in 1836. By 1851, Bond was living in a house called 'Old Quay House', and from the above details it would not surprise me if this was where he was living at the time the letter was written.

When the contents of the house were sold following Bond's death in early January 1858, the contents listed were reminiscent of those you would have expected inside Ashton Lodge, the home of the bankers, the aforementioned Pedder. All the furniture was of mahogany construction, with the dining-room chairs, a sideboard, and four carved bed-post pillars all being described as 'massive.'

Also, in the mid-1840s he formed an association with James M. Nelson, who operated as Nelson's Vessels out of the Port of Liverpool and carrying on the sort of business that Bond had declared an interest in, the importing and exporting of wines and spirits. Within a short period of time, Bond is advertising as the Liverpool Preston Steam Navigation Company, and suggesting in the notice that James M. Nelson had 'left the company.' A letter to the same paper, signed by Nelson, made an allegation of 'an ingenious device' being worked against him, in order to take his trade, but William sailed on.

Around twelve months earlier, William Bond and a group of other contractors, brought to a successful conclusion, negotiations to build a bonded warehouse on what was known as the New Quay, and stood around fifty yards from the River Ribble. It is necessary to recall that at this time the river ran along its original course, and was only later altered and straightened, when the docks were constructed towards the end of the nineteenth century.

The foundation stone for the bonded warehouses was laid in February 1844 in the presence of a number of corporation officials, contractors, and many lady guests. Flags aplenty were fluttering from the temporary erections on the quay, among which was a very handsome one, belonging to Mr. Bond, and bearing the inscription "Success to the Ribble," and at two o'clock, the foundation stone was hoisted in a hod in readiness, while the Lord Mayor, John Addison, addressed those gathered for the event. He pointed out that Preston had been a port from ancient times, and, according to tradition, the chief magistrate of the town was, in those days, called the 'Portreeve' or Port Warden, a position that no longer existed. Since those times, the river had become silted up, rendering Preston less important as a trading centre.

The recent work of the Ribble Navigation Company had, in great measure, removed those obstacles, and trade was again beginning to grow. He informed the gathering that Her Majesty's government had renewed privileges attached to Preston being a significant port and, in recognition of that, it was intended to name the new buildings, the Victoria Warehouses.

By the November of 1853, our ship-owning, wines, and spirits importing, William Bond, had erected the magnificent building that many of us knew as the Port Admiral Hotel. On the twelfth of that month, a celebratory dinner was held in the building. Chief among the guests were the contractors who had been responsible for its construction, and about seventy of the workmen who had undertaken it, and the festivities went a considerable way to enhance Mr. Bond's reputation of generosity. Certainly an edifice, but was it a memorial to this hard-working, ambitious, generous, although some may say ruthless individual. He had died by January 1858 aged 53 years. Had he had a premonition? We do not know, and probably never will, but the magnificent Longridge stone building, literally smothered with the work of his craftsmen, and possibly others, gives every appearance of a memorial. Each storey had its own stone carvings, as well as the area immediately below the roofline, all intricately carved. The roof itself had four carved lions at each corner, and atop a raised plinth on the front of the building were three larger than life-size statues.

It has long been accepted that the lady in the centre, whose lack of bodily coverings gave rise to some unsavoury names for the hotel, was a likeness of Lady Hamilton, a lady with a connection to the town. However, many experts in such things have said that there is no material difference between it, and a selection of other Greek Maiden statues. There have also been suggestions that the second man was Sir William Hamilton, but I see no reason why he should have been deserving of such an honour, particularly when his second wife, Lady Emma Hamilton, was famed as Horatio Nelson's mistress! If this is where the story about Lady Hamilton arose, then I am tempted to dismiss both as mere myths. She was simply a copy of a statue called 'The Greek Slave,' sculpted by Hiram Powers, and exhibited at the Great Exhibition at the Crystal Palace in 1851, and replicated by one of his tradesmen two years later.

One of the men was said to be a likeness of Lord Nelson, which it certainly was, and when the building was demolished in 1969, the statue was taken by the brewery to another of their houses, the Trafalgar Hotel, in Nelson, East Lancashire. I am afraid that the Trafalgar is now an Asian supermarket, and nobody knows the current whereabouts of Lord Nelson.

I recall at the time the hotel was demolished, a man I knew who was involved in the antiques trade, Hermon Hambleton, bought a snake and two of the rooftop lions. He had a penchant for things connected with Preston and would have willingly bought the three main statues had the brewery not intervened. The two lions enjoyed their retirement at ground level in a garden in Ashton, and the snake enjoyed the sunshine on its back in a Fulwood garden.

Despite the fact that the hotel spent its entire existence in the belief that the third figure was a representation of Napolean Bonaparte, and since it was demolished no one has disputed it, I have reason to believe that the third figure was the Duke of Wellington. Where else is there a statue of the vanquished? Soon after the hotel was erected, Lancashire writer and poet Edwin Waugh was taken on a tour of Preston, and among the features shown him were the statues, with the third person described as the Duke of Wellington, and the other two as Nelson and a Greek Slave. It has been suggested that the pose, with one hand inside the tunic is an indication that it must be Bonaparte, but I have seen images of Wellington in such a pose as well.

Left: A painting of the Duke of Wellington, showing his right arm supported within his uniform.

Right: An image of Napolean, also with his right arm supported

Left: Removed from their plinth at the front of the Port Admiral, the trio of statues are admired by the men of Chris Miller haulage, whilst at the same time, carefully preserving the Greek Maidens' modesty.

At some point prior to 1851, Bond had bought the Ship Inn at Marsh End, and for a period lived there and ran it. It was in almost the same position as its successor, the New Ship Inn on Watery Lane, a house that has had an unremarkable recent history, but during the hey-day of Preston Docks, along with many other neighbouring inns and taverns, carried on a thriving business with sailors from most parts and ports of the world.

Following the death of William Bond in January 1859, an auction was held at the Port Admiral Hotel, for the purpose of disposing of his substantial assets, contained in five Lots. Lot One was the Ship Inn, in the occupation of John Paley, and the seven adjoining properties. The second and third Lots consisted of sixteen dwellings in Dover Street and North Road. The fourth Lot was the Port Admiral, together with the brewhouse and stables, all of which were in the occupation of James Gardner, the only person to have run the business by that time, and seven adjoining dwelling-houses, plus one in Saul Street and six on High Street. William Bond had accumulated a substantial property portfolio indeed.

Returning to the hotel's brief cinematic experience, the questionable details emerged following an article in the *Lancashire Daily Post* in 1933, where it was stated that the first motion pictures were shown in London in 1896. Mr. J. Airey, of Miller Street, Preston, wrote to the paper claiming that it was he who showed the first motion pictures, not in London, but in a cellar in Bank Hey Street, Blackpool, and shortly afterwards, in Preston, in 1895.

He went on to say that it was in the large, first floor room of the Port Admiral Hotel where he showed the films in Preston, adding that the landlord's name was Mr. Jackson. Furthermore, he explained that there were three self-produced films which lasted about an hour in total, that he was paid for his attendance, but the audience were allowed in free of charge, on the basis that the landlord's reward would be from the sale of intoxicants to the attendees.

The outcome was less lucrative than it might well have been hoped because a complaint was made regarding the commotion on Lancaster Road, created by those congregating in the hope of admission. The crowd was quickly dispersed by police who visited from the police station in Earl Street, barely 150 yards distant.

The following day he went to Bolton, where the projector that he had bought from an American who could not work out how to use it, was sold.

I have little doubt that the event took place, but I have to question the year that it occurred. George Jackson did not become the landlord until 1898, and he died a year later, so if he was the landlord, it would fix the year at that one. Furthermore, there had been three other landlords between 1895 and 1898, so it is unlikely that the name has been confused.

In cinematic history, 1895 was extremely early, and any moving images would be very different to what we may imagine, but I am reliably informed by David J. Hindle, and referred to in his Victorian Preston book (2012), that this sort of entertainment was being offered, generally by travelling showmen and often in temporary, circus-like structures. The Preston paper's reference to him being 'known among his fellow showmen as Professor Baldhead,' together with association with Blackpool, may suggest that he was among their kinship.

Little else is known about Mr. Airey, other than in the same article, he claimed that he was the first person in Britain to open a fried fish shop on Friargate in Preston in 1874/75, before opening others in Adelphi Street, Moor Lane, and Park Road. He retired in 1920, after 45 years in the trade, which included a period just five years less, at 40 years, as the agent for the Fish Friers' Association of the district, when he responded to a complaint from the Manx Fisheries Association about fish friers profiteering. At the time, portions of fried fish were being sold at 3d or 4d (less than 2p), and the complaint never gained traction.

The *Lancashire Daily Post* also revealed that he had other things to which he claimed to be the first person to achieve them, for example that he was the first person to use a phonograph on Blackpool sands, earning money from ten customers at a time who were listening on earphones. He also claimed to be the first person to take cinematic films, and develop them in a bucket and finally, that he was the first to take tin ferrotype pictures, sometimes called tintype, also on Blackpool sands. Unfortunately, those brief, tantalising hints at other facets of the man's life have produced nothing in the way of detail.

However, anybody who claims to have been the first to achieve so many 'firsts' in his life, must have had an element of showman in him?

The Black Horse Hotel

Friargate

The Black Horse Hotel in Friargate could be Preston's best-known hostelry. There are several aspects of it that may come as a surprise to many, including those who have frequented it over the years. Perhaps the most universally accepted fact about it is that it is the only public house in the United Kingdom with three entrances on different streets, and therefore, having three addresses. I believe they were all registered with the postal services at one time. In addition to 167, Friargate, you may also address your Christmas cards to 1, Orchard Street and 1, Plant's Court, Rowland Plant's Court, or as the latter has also been known variously over the years as Black Horse Yard and Lowthian Street. Whatever you choose to call it, the passage can still be traversed from Orchard Street as far as the side of the Market Hotel on Market Street. I am sure that there are many, like me, who can recall walking through the Hippodrome entrance foyer from Friargate, to join the passage at around the halfway point, whilst making their way to Starch House Square, which in my case was to catch the 'bus to school.

From the beginning of the 19th Century, Preston had many quaint yards and courts running off the main thoroughfares, and a great many of those, like Lowthian Street, ran off Friargate. The alternative name of Plant's Court was derived from a woman and her husband solicitor, Rowland, in Preston. In 1786, Joseph Sudell and Ellen Plant, sold a private dwelling to George Sim. It had previously been an inn known as the Hoop and Crown, and was later to be returned to such use, bearing the same name. It stood at 161 Friargate, just six doors from the Black Horse Hotel, a property you will discover was sold by, presumably, the same George Sim just eleven years later in 1797.

Above: When it was rebuilt in 1898, it was the tallest licensed premises in the borough of Preston. (Photo: Dan Taylor)

At that time, the Hoop and Crown had a connection to the rear with the passage that would later acquire the name Plant's Court, although after the erection of the Hippodrome Theatre, the connection was lost. Whatever, in 1739, after John Colley, owner of Colley's Gardens, later to become Starch House Square, was summoned before the Court Leet with regards his failure to keep the passage in good repair, and for some time afterwards it was referred to colloquially as 'Dirty Alley'.

Almost a century later, in 1838, a start was made to enlarge the passage from Friargate into Lowthian Street to form Orchard Street, and to take its course towards Chadwick's Orchard, the place where the Covered Market now stands. I will mention that again in a moment, but I find it ironical that an alternative route was proposed along with this one, of linking Friargate with Back Lane, now Market Street. That plan was to demolish buildings opposite the entrance to Lune Street, and access Back Lane from there. The same access point became, in the second half of the 20th Century, a part of Ringway, our inner-city by-pass, a road that many consider divides the town into two parts.

It is a common misconception that the Black Horse is an ancient inn, because the one that we now know was only constructed in 1898. The architect was John A. Seward, a 43-year-old Lancaster born man who lived in Higher Road, Longridge, and he designed the building for the Kay's Atlas Brewery Company of Manchester. It is now owned by Robinson's Brewery of Stockport.

However, its forerunner, on the same site, has a history going back to at least 1797, when it was still known as the Black Horse. At times during the intervening years, it was also known as the Black Horse and Rainbow, and for a portion of those years, Orchard Street did not even exist. There was a narrow entrance to the side of the hotel that followed the course of the passage we still refer to as Lowthian Street, and next to the building that for many of us will forever be referred to as 'The Umbrella Shop'. Despite its odd, angular shape, it was once operated as a beerhouse called the Market Tavern, but for many years it was the brewhouse for the Black Horse Hotel. The cellars for it are believed to be under Lowthian Street, and further, that the cellars of the Black Horse are also, adding evidence to a link between the two places.

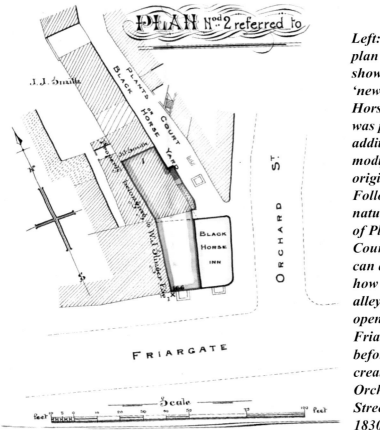

PLAN Nᵒᵈ 2 referred to

Left: This plan clearly shows how the 'new' Black Horse Hotel was purely an addition to the modified original. Following the natural course of Plant's Court, you can discern how the alleyway opened onto Friargate before the creation of Orchard Street in the 1830s.

In the 1940s, Preston Herald reporter, J. H. Spencer, recorded that there had always been a suggestion that the original part of the Black Horse had, between 1768 and 1792, been the Preston house of General John Burgoyne, the British General, dramatist, and politician, who sat in the House of commons from 1761 until 1792. He was elected as the Whig MP for Preston in 1768.

Above: The acutely angled corner of what used to be the Market Tavern can be seen to the right of Lowthian Street / Black Horse Yard. (Photo: David Toase)

In 1797, ownership passed from George Sims the Younger, a cabinet maker, to James Gregson of Walton-le-dale, a cotton manufacturer, for the princely sum of £300, at a time when Thomas Holmes was described in the transaction as 'being in possession or occupation of', in his position as landlord. He had been there for an unknown period, but nothing else is known about its history. For many years, the Black Horse after it was rebuilt, operated as a residential hotel, and taking advantage of the neighbouring Royal Hippodrome, which opened in 1905. It has been suggested that there was a 'private' passageway from the theatre directly to the Black Horse, but it may have been from the Stage Door, a few paces along Lowthian Street, to the third entrance to the hotel.

I was witness to an amusing incident that happened in the early 1970s when the landlord was Jack Whalley, a bow-tied, dapper gentleman who took his innkeeping seriously. One cold, winter evening, the Friargate door opened and a man who had clearly had far too much to drink, staggered in. Jack approached the man, told him he had had enough to drink, and to make his way home. He left, but within a minute or two, re-appeared through the Orchard Street entrance, with Jack repeating his request. Two minutes later he made his third and final appearance through the Lowthian Street doorway, but before Jack could utter a word, the man asked him "How many pubs have you got?"

Nothing is known about the appearance of the original Black Horse, but the new one is Grade II listed. Many Grade II listings relate to a particular feature or features, but in this case, it relates to the building's exterior and interior in its entirety. It is a red brick building with sandstone dressings, and the slate roof made this three-storey building the tallest public house structure in Preston in 1898, a time when the Preston Improvement Act was implementing improvements to benefit the visual appearance of many parts of the town centre.

The outside of the building is full of interest, provided by the rooms on all three floors on the corner with Orchard Street, with canted bays to the first and second storey, both overlooking Friargate, and with returns that overlook Orchard Street. The room on the first floor was known as Peter's Bar, the name of which perplexed many visitors, certainly until the mid-1970s, and maybe as long as it existed. I will explain later.

Both the Friargate and Orchard Street entrance doorways have beautiful elliptical-headed, moulded stones, each with a horse's head in a central position. At the side of the Friargate stone are two substantial stone brackets which feature stone carvings of male and female figures, and which carry above them a balustraded balcony.

The mosaic floor in the entrance below carries the name of the hotel and leads to a further mosaic floored passage leading to the main body of the pub which is centred around the servery. Along that

passage are two doors with glass panels announcing them as Smoke Rooms, and despite their irrelevance, they remain marked as such.

Whilst the exterior has remained unaltered since 1898, and in many ways can be described as unique, the interior can claim almost the same longevity and irreplaceability, and is most certainly, unique. Its appearance remains almost unaltered, including the central bar which, in part, is semi-circular and elaborately tiled. This single feature, together with the accompanying intricate floor mosaics, are the features to which visitors flock from far and wide. It has been described as reflective of not only the Arts and Crafts period which was at its height between 1880 and 1920, but also the movement that it was to inspire, Art Nouveau, which began slightly later around 1890, and was dominant until about 1920. 'Stepping back in time' can be a somewhat hackneyed phrase but walking through any of the three doors of this hostelry cannot be described in any other way.

The tiled dado rail of light brown plain tiles, with a selection of red and light blue decorative tiled panels, the ornately plastered ceilings, the copper door furniture, and a host of original joinery and pieces of stained-glass work, provide a sensory overload for the interested observer. Even the seating has remained unaltered since 1929. Every nook and cranny remain unaltered since its Victorian roots.

The elaborate mosaic floor is, according to Historic England, consistent with that sort of flooring for 1898, yet there is a common belief that the tiling was the work of the Stockport company, Quiligottis. It could be that over the years, repair work or renovations have been carried out by them, but the company, founded by an Italian immigrant, was only begun in about 1945, after a short period of constructing air-raid shelters.

The ceramic tiled semi-circular bar is the feature that is particular well known, and in many ways, unique. CAMRA, the Campaign for Real Ale, in their wonderful description of the Black Horse, recorded that it was possibly the work of Pilkington Ceramics, 'in its graceful cream and light green with its bulging pilasters, decorative brackets and wooden top'. They add that, 'There are only fourteen ceramic bar counters left in the country, widely spread, but with one in the Burlington bar at the Town House, St. Annes-on-Sea. There is a further school of thought that suggests that the bar tiling is the work of Burmantoft's, a Leeds company, with their faience (tin glazed) style of tiling.

Above: Whoever was responsible for the tiling on the circular bar, it remains the feature that attracts visitors from far and wide. (Photo: David Toase)

Peter's Bar in the late 1960s, was the place to take a new girlfriend, for there was a feeling of exclusivity about being able to make your way up the stairs, to find your way to the front, elevated lounge. In summer, there seemed something avant garde about drinking one's beer, with your lady sipping her Babycham (the addition of a glazed cherry was mandatory), whilst simultaneously gazing through the bay window at the passing pedestrians. In the depths of winter, the heavy curtains helped to provide a warm and comfortable surrounding for its guests. Why it was called Peter's Bar was a question I never heard answered with certainty, but when I began delving into the history of our inns and taverns, I discovered that one of the first licensees after the place was rebuilt was John Samuel Peters. He died in early 1904, and I suspect that for whatever reason, the room remembered his name and presence from then onwards.

Sarah Hannah Peters was to endure more than just grief, for after two years running the Black Horse alone, she married Frederick

Tunney, a musician by trade or profession. Within six weeks he had become a habitual user of the bar facilities, which caused him to become abusive and violent. Many were the beatings suffered by Frederick's new bride, treatment she put up with in silence, but after six months of such behaviour, and a particular threat to throttle and throw her down the stairs, she summoned him for his assaults and abusive behaviour. Surprisingly, the court decided that there was insufficient evidence to convict, and the case was dismissed.

What happened between them after that is not known, but each year, she placed 'In Memorium' notices in the local press until at least 1920 relating to John Peters, and she remained as the landlady until 1922. However, when she died, at the age of 67 years in 1935, the notice of her death read, "Sarah Hannah (Sally) the beloved wife of Frederick Tunney." There are so many alternative stories of their lives that could cover the intervening thirty years, but I am afraid I do not know what the correct one would be.

Although it is true that beneath the streets of Preston, there is a labyrinth of tunnels, and a former licensee at the Black Horse told me that at one time it was possible to walk from his cellar to a position on Plungington Road around Ripon Street. Most of these tunnels are now bricked up at various points along their lengths. They must have had a practical use at some point in our history, but at the same time, they are probably the cause of several myths. Or perhaps they were not myths? Perhaps they were used by people to move round the town unnoticed, without it being the original purpose of them. Could this have been the means by which entertainers moved unnoticed from the Hippodrome to the Black Horse?

It is known that Preston was built on the top of a hill that rose from the river to the south and east of it, and although it has now spread to consume all the lower land around it, the whole of the town centre is well above sea level. In 1864, riverside public houses suffered immense flood damage in torrential rain and swollen rivers, but in the May of that year, even the Black Horse Hotel became a sufferer following a hailstorm, with the water produced by it forcing large quantities of sand in addition to five feet of water, into the cellar. All open barrels were lost, and the bungs of many other barrels were forced out under the pressure and consequently lost. A brew of ale that was working in the back cellar was upset, washed away, and lost. The stillage which previously supported the barrels ended on top of the barrels, and men worked until three o'clock the following morning to remove the sand, filling four carts, before any repairs could be contemplated.

The landlord at the time of the flooding was Joseph Pritt. It was a rather inauspicious beginning for him, having only recently moved into the hotel. Joseph Pritt, a man who was part of a talented and artistic family, was better known for more than his innkeeping. He was the producer of ceremonial flags and banners that were in big demand, and typical of church, school and Sunday school, and trade organisation processions at particularly the annual Whitsuntide processions, and even more widely during those of Preston Guild Weeks.

Finally, whilst looking for information about the Atlas Brewery Company, who owned the Black Horse before Robinson's of Stockport bought it from them, I came across a similarly named Atlas Brewing Company. I noticed that the Orkney Islands were mentioned, and was intrigued, for I have a soft spot for Scottish islands, so I looked further. Gone maybe are the days when beer arrived on a carriage drawn by a couple of majestic Shire horses, but for a carriage fee of around £12, you can now have a couple of Mini Casks of Orkney beers, with evocative names such as Dark Island and Northern Light, delivered directly to your door from the Atlas Brewing Company of today!

The Arms of The Spinners and The Spindlemakers.

Lancaster Road

Above: The original Spindlemakers' Arms, featured on an advertising postcard. Published by the son of the first landlord, James B. Dobson.

Standing barely one hundred metres apart on Lancaster Road, these two inns would seem to beg comparisons and yet present contrasts simultaneously. I recently saw on social media that someone claimed to have had their first pint in the Spinners' Arms, but even if that had been as an underage sixteen-year-old, they would have had, at the time of the comment, to be 117 years old! More likely, they have confused it with the Spindlemakers' Arms, a popular destination through to the 1970s and 1980s.

From a local historian's point of view, both houses have offered much interest, and particularly in relation to how they acquired their names. Many names related to their first landlord and the trade he or she had followed, for instance the short-lived Coopers' Arms on Bridge Street, now part of Marsh Lane. I will mention that one again in the final chapter of this book.

In the case of the Spindlemakers' Arms, I was contacted by a descendant of the first landlord, John Dobson, who took residence there in 1849. John's wife, Elizabeth, was a native of Caton in the Lune valley, where her father, John Proctor, was the local spindlemaker. "Do you think that could be the reason for how the pub got its name?" I was asked. Well, you can come to your own conclusion, but in my mind, there is no question at all. I feel certain it is. John Proctor moved to Preston, and lived close by.

The Enumerator's Census of 1851 revealed that the Spinners' Arms had already opened its doors, and it is less of a surprise that the first residents had a history in the cotton spinning trade. I am sure that the many taverns that carry the sign of a trade, are worthy of closer investigation to establish whether there is a similar link.

Remaining at the Spinners' Arms for a while because it closed in 1919, its position in Lancaster Road remained unclear. I knew roughly where it was but had no reason to investigate further. I was contacted by a lady whose ancestral family had played a part in several public houses in Preston, including the Spinners', and she also was trying to establish its position. She went through a steep learning curve during her search, as indeed all local historians will agree is necessary before real progress can be made. A search she had made on 'Google Earth' for 61 Lancaster Road had revealed that it was somewhere between the covered market and the new Crown Court building on the opposite side of Ringway. Modern technology undoubtedly has huge benefits, but what it did not understand on this occasion was that at one time there was a Lancaster Road South, and a Lancaster Road North, with the Spinners' being in the latter; and in any event, street numbering has altered more than once.

I discovered a sale notice in a Preston Chronicle of 1890, where 'a block of twelve houses, plus the Spinners' Arms,' were offered for sale, describing them as 'close to St. Thomas's Church.' It further mentioned that the block consisted of two houses and the Spinners' Arms on Lancaster Road, and five houses each in side streets adjacent to the property on Lancaster Road. Five houses were in Ousby Street, and a similar number in Appleby Street, the next street further north. St. Thomas's Church stands on the corner of Appleby Street, and so it and the tavern were next door neighbours.

A fortnight before the sale notice, a story appeared in the Lancashire Evening Post, relating to the illegal selling of intoxicants by the inhabitants of number one Appleby Street. Their yard wall formed a division between that property and the Spinners' Arms. Two policemen had been suspicious of activity at number one Appleby Street, and when they saw a lady leave the house on a Sunday morning, they stopped her and found two bottles of ale under her shawl. They took her back to the house, where she pointed to the occupant and said, "I paid her for it." The occupant, who we can, by this time describe as the defendant, replied, "Yes, you gave me a shilling last night."

On searching the premises, the policemen found in the back yard, a hole in the dividing wall, about nine inches square. The hole opened into the yard of the Spinners' Arms. It is not often that such detail comes to light, leaving no doubt as to where a property was positioned, but here we have it with certainty.

Right: A surveyors bench mark inlaid into the church wall (see map below). The horizontal line indicates the height above sea level that line is, and when used in conjunction with other bench marks, it is possible to calculate all heights in between. The height at this point is indicated on the map on the next page, and shown in feet.

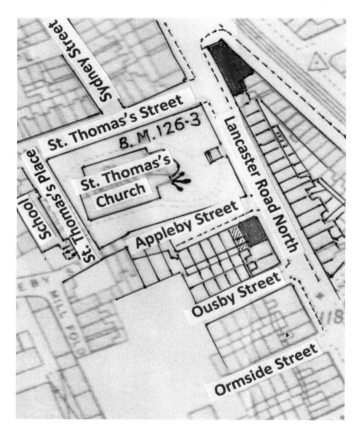

Above: The Spinners' Arms and its yard are marked in red, with number 1, Appleby Street adjacent to the hatched area. The building marked blue, was the Church Hotel in its prominent position at the confluence of North Road and Lancaster Road North. It was at the Church Hotel that attendees at St. Thomas's could find stabling for their horses. In Sydney Street East, at its junction with Back Sydney Street, was a beerhouse with the delightful name of 'The Ocean Monarch'. You can read more about that in the final chapter of this book.

The B.M. (Benchmark) in the grounds of the church, was the pre-GPS method of levelling for surveyors, showing the interesting information that we are, at the point of the arrow engraved into the sandstone building, 126.3 feet above sea level.

In 1909 a dynasty came to an end when George Sandiford, the landlord of the Spinners' Arms at that time, sold the business after his family had been there for forty years. The name Sandiford only appeared thirty years before that date, so whether their predecessors, the Singletons' and the Gregsons' were linked by marriage remain to be established. It did, however, continue in the same family, for George's brother Alfred, bought the business, and remained until 1917, just two years before it finally closed its doors, when his wife Florence was still recorded as the owner.

The 1890 advertisement already referred to, also mentioned that the premises were leasehold for 999 years from 2nd February 1835, which begs the question as to whether the premises had been operated under a different name from that date until the Spinners' Arms was first recorded in 1851. Its neighbour, St. Thomas's Church, the handsome, sandstone, Norman-style church, was built between 1837 and 1839.

Above: The most recent of the Spindlemakers' Arms, has remained closed since the early 1990s.

Continuous family possession of the Spindlemakers' Arms is evident here as well, but is much clearer, in terms of both the licence and the property. Elizabeth, the widow of John, the original owner, was in possession of it until almost the close of the 19th century, when, in the first half of the 1890s, possession passed to her son, John Bramwell Dobson, who, at the age of about forty, retired from a teaching career to take over in this undoubtedly thriving business.

When a licensed house remains in the same family over a long period, it is a certain indication that it's a profitable one, and when John Bramwell Dobson arrived, it needed to be, for he still had eight of his nine children living with him. During the previous sixteen years he had been living at the School House, in the remote hamlet of Rusland, near Satterthwaite, in the idyllic Rusland Valley, close to Grizedale, an area between Coniston Water and Windermere, which was still in Lancashire at that time.

Another benefit of a long-term, family-owned licensed business, is that they tend to be trouble free, and particularly so in terms of discipline and behaviour within the premises, and consequent police attention.

At the end of the century, in 1897, and only a few years into their tenure, worry and sadness was to visit the Dobson's household, when their seventeen year old daughter, Elizabeth, was, in the words of the *Blackburn Weekly Standard* in 1899, seduced by three youths who had started to frequent the Spindlemakers' Arms immediately prior to the incident.

As a result of the attack, Elizabeth became pregnant, and in late 1897 gave birth to a son, but the incident did not make the press until 1899 when John Bramwell Dobson made a civil claim for damages against the three individuals, claiming compensation for the loss of her earnings over an extensive period, resulting in a need to employ somebody in her place. Not only was Elizabeth responsible for the housekeeping in the property, but she also had duties as a barmaid. She had been quite ill as a result of her experiences, and spent a period in the Southport Sanatorium. He was awarded £75.

It is of interest that none of the youths were prosecuted for any offence, and I am inclined to believe that the majority of Elizabeth's first seventeen years were in the backwaters of the Lake District, and that this naïve young lady was, maybe, unprepared for life in an ever-growing industrial town. I would have been reluctant to include this story, but I am aware that descendants alive today are aware of what happened over one hundred years ago.

There were two periods when a name other than Dobson was at the helm at the Spindlemakers. In 1871, Thomas Coup appeared in the Census of that year, but it isn't clear how long he remained; and in 1892, Hugh Gibson was the licensee for a short period prior to the arrival of James Bramwell Dobson.

What is certain, is that they were managers, because the property, as we have seen, still remained with the Dobson's, with ownership passing to James Bramwell Dobson in around 1895, with a further continuation in about 1915, when eldest son, William, a tin-plate worker, who had been living with his family in the Adelphi Street, Moor Lane area, became the fourth member of the dynasty to hold the license, following the death of his father.

The descendant of the Dobson's, with whom I have corresponded tells me that William Dobson's younger brother, James, was also involved in the running of the Spindlemakers' Arms after their father's death, and although their departure definitely brought an end to the dynasty of family ownership, there is no certainty when, other than it was by 1926, a date that would have meant seventy-seven years in the possession of one family.

Above: The Grey Horse and Seven Stars Inn, Fishergate,
viewed from Cannon Street

Grey Horses – White Horses

A Stable Full of Horses

When you stop and think about our local past, the horse, as our most faithful servant will not be too far away from those thoughts. From the packhorse to the stagecoach, there was a connecting link between the two entities. Was it not Shakespeare's Richard III who uttered the phrase, "A horse! A Horse! My kingdom for a horse!?" Many a regular and experienced a traveller would have remembered their indebtedness to their steed and the inns and taverns they visited at the end of each leg of what would have been arduous journeys.

It is little wonder that Preston, being at the hub of a traveller's journey for millennia to the present day, that it is well represented in our extensive acknowledgment to our four-legged equestrian friends.

We have had horses of black, white, bay, and grey named on our inn signs, to say nothing of one that could fly. A Horse and Farrier stood in Melling Street, off North Road, which was later better known as 'Scragg's', for the combination of Stephen Senior, and son, Albert, the name Scragg was over the door as licensee for the better part of fifty years.

Earlier, there had been another Horse and Farrier in Tithebarn Street, but people will only recall it as the Market Hotel, the name to which it was changed around 1850. It faced the top of Lord Street, and for many it was always referred to "As the pub next door to Molly Johnson's flat meat and potato pie shop!" When it first opened there was a pork market next door on the corner of Lord's Walk, rendering the renaming of the hotel simple. For a little in excess of ten years, the name of the hotel was temporarily changed to The Lady of the Lake. It was the name of a play by Sir Walter Scott, dramatized at our Theatre Royal more than once, but it was also the name of a racehorse that was owned by the landlord, Robert Atkinson, who took over the hotel in 1848. Despite changes of tenancy, it retained the name until 1859 when it reverted to Market Hotel. Atkinson had previously been the landlord of the Sir Walter Scott Inn at the junction of North Road and Lord's Walk.

Across the road from the Market Hotel was the Waggon and Horses, latterly known as the Tithebarn Hotel. Its reputation rarely flattered the establishment, and often related to its clientele, and a far cry from the days when opera singing was practiced on Sunday evenings, along with a selection of hymns. An even lesser number will know that it was once known as The Stocking, or The Volunteer, both gleaned from legal documents that included a plan of the footprint of the premises and showing the uniquely angled pavement line that I now know has existed for at least 224 years, as the pavement leads from Tithebarn Street into Lord Street. I also have reason to believe that before any of the names I have mentioned, it was known as The Setting Dog.

There was a Horse Shoe Hotel in Church Street which, in about 1922 changed its name to the George Hotel when the hotel of that name at the junction of Friargate and Market Street gave up its licence and opened as a bank. It was a popular rendez-vous of prison officers, and the combination of them and long-serving licensees, Jim, and Belle Webster, who ran a no-nonsense public house, were able to welcome trusted prisoners who were allowed out a couple of nights a week as part of their programme of rehabilitation into society. The George Hotel has now been consumed by its neighbour, Ted Carter's fishing tackle empire, and now serves as a warehouse for them. I discovered a further Horse Shoe, a beerhouse in Back Lane, now Market Street West, in 1841, but like many a beerhouse it may have been a fleeting attempt to start a business, or it had been known as something else either before or after that date.

Pack Horses were recognized with two taverns carrying their name. One existed on the lower part of Walker Street for around sixty years, disappearing in about 1930. A second one persisted ten years longer, before closing, along with many others, in 1907, having opened its doors in the 1830s. It was in Heatley Street, and stood on the corner of Seed Street a few strides from the New Britannia.

The name Doctor Syntax does not immediately suggest that a horse is being referred to, but it is; and a very special horse it was too. The two taverns that carried its name on their signs can be read about in the final chapter of this book.

Returning to the variously coloured horses, important features on an inn sign at a time when few could read, let us begin with the Grey Horse and Seven Stars on Fishergate, where the Lancashire Evening Post offices stood. It had existed since before 1820, but did not acquire its astronomical appendage until 1845, and there are those who suggest that it had previously been known as the White Horse, but the sign had dulled to a grey colour, and rather than paint the sign they renamed the pub! It may be observed that I am not convinced with that account, but what I know for certain is that there was a White Horse on the opposite side of Fishergate that had its rear-facing windows overlooking what we now know as Winckley Square parkland. The property was owned and run by William Hudson, and directly next door to it moving towards the town centre, was an inn called The Wheatsheaf in the care of Robert Carr. So much to discover, and so many myths to dispel. The 1732 Poor Law Rate Assessment Book refers to William Hudson of the White Horse and Seven Stars on Fishergate, so I am not at all convinced that the later change of name for the Grey Horse was entirely original.

Shortly after the seven silver stars had been painted on a bright blue background, and beyond an impressive grey horse, a description that I am thankful for, because it is not something I have seen in real life, the inn was taken over by William Hardwick, who was the son of another William who had been the landlord from 1832 until his death in 1836. William Hardwick Senior was also the father of the rather better-known Charles Hardwick, a man who wrote a history of Preston, as well as being a talented artist and oil-painter. A notable feature on the pavement by the entrance was an old horse-mounting stone that had been there many years.

In 1852, William Hardwick left the Grey Horse and Seven Stars, and became a maltster in a well-known brewing area of the town close to Lark Hill, off Manchester Road, and it was while he was there that a monkey that he had as a pet, died. The following is an account of the bond formed between the monkey and a terrier dog, while in Hardwick's possession.

The following is the transcript of an article in the Preston Guardian of the 17th of December 1853.

The Extraordinary Affection Between a Monkey and a Terrier.

A fine East-Indian monkey, the property of Mr. William Hardwick, maltster, Lark Hill, died a few days ago. "Mr. Jerry" as he was called, formed during his life an extensive range of acquaintances, and was, three or four years ago, occasionally on rather too familiar terms with several respectable tradesmen on the north side of Fishergate, adjacent to the Grey Horse, whose patience he tested with his tricks and destructive tendencies. On more than one occasion, a shot gun has been levelled at him as he amused himself on the Fishergate rooftops, distributing slates into the roadway, but he always managed to avoid injury.

Hardwick had, eight or nine years earlier, been given the monkey by a relative, as an acknowledgement for something William had carried out for them. It is doubtful whether it was a gift that he was happy to receive, but he determined that, if possible, he would try to rear the animal. In his early attempts to introduce the newly named "Mr. Jerry" to the other animal in the household, a white, rough-haired English terrier bitch, named "Fan," the meetings were met with an assortment of snarling's and snapping's, and on the odd occasion, battles-royal. His attempts to encourage "Fan" to become stepmother to the young "Mr. Jerry" were not met with instant success.

Perseverance is a useful quality, and quite soon the two found they could live in harmony, and for many years were chained to the same kennel at the rear of the Grey Horse and Seven Stars, with the monkey learning to cope with the worrying propensities of Fan. They had their occasional squabbles, but they were passed off as merely an imitation of their owners!

With this particular pairing, it was quickly realised that "Mr. Jerry" was the one with the brains, and "Fan" the one that possessed the brawn, and there were anecdotal tales which would indicate a greater amount of calculating purpose and sound judgement than could be put down merely to instinct. One of those instances requires you to imagine the scene at the rear of the pub, where the kennel was housed in the open area below a flight of steps, with the monkey accessing the kennel from the steps, onto the top of a five feet tall door, and dropping down into the kennel. On one particular occasion a mischievous person or persons, fixed several nails to the inside of the door, with the consequence that when "Mr. Jerry" leapt from the steps, onto the door, and down into the kennel, his chain became caught on one of the nails, leaving him dangling in mid-air. It was only successful on one occasion! He quickly regained his position on top of the door, made a study of the cause of his entanglement, carefully retraced his steps, and coolly unhooked the chain from the nail. Returning to his position on the top of the door, he hauled up the chain like an experience seaman. He then re-entered the kennel, leaving no slack in the chain to become caught. It was said that on reaching the ground he emitted what was described as a 'crackling chatter of triumphant defiance'.

On another occasion, this time in the bar of the Grey Horse, a visiting gentleman who had been amused by some of the monkey's antics, determined that he would 'stand' the monkey a glass of rum. Immediately the monkey formed his hand into the shape of a spoon, and successfully transferred the rum to his mouth. Two more glasses appeared, and it was said, by the servant of the house, that "Mr. Jerry" became 'glorious, and staggered and reeled like any "drunken Christian". Whether it was the headache of the following day or not, and despite never signing any pledges, it was a prank that was never repeated, for "Mr. Jerry" had learned his lesson! His love of lettuce had not passed the notice of one mischievous person, who sprinkled paprika on a leaf. The grotesque look of dissatisfaction on the monkey's face could hardly be mistaken for a grin, and never again did he eat a lettuce leaf without inspecting it closely for any foreign body.

If "Mr. Jerry" had any behavioural faults, perhaps it was his selfishness at mealtimes with his friend "Fan". I do not suppose that it is Jerry's fault that monkeys, and dogs are physiologically different, but it did give him the added bonus of being able to retain in his mouth all the dainty and tasty morsels, storing them at great speed, until the time arrived to chew them thoroughly for final consumption.

On the odd occasion "Mr. Jerry" would escape from his chain and make his way into the bedrooms of neighbouring properties, with combs, brushes, hand-mirrors and even bottles of Eau-de-Cologne, being ejected onto Fishergate. Closed and even locked windows were seen as minor inconveniences when entry to the house would be gained by removing a slate or two. He was even known to gain entry down a chimney occasionally, to the terror of the housemaid.

During the early part of December 1853, Mr. Hardwick awoke to find his terrier, "Fan," clearly dying, with "Mr. Jerry" standing over her making a strange, moaning noise. Shortly afterwards, "Fan" breathed her last, and from that very moment, the monkey could not be distracted from her general moping behaviour. As the dog was buried between two cherry trees, the monkey began what was described as a dismal howl, and although every conceivable effort made to distract him, he refused to associate with any other animal, or to eat. Just four days later, he died, and was buried in the same grave as his foster-mother and faithful companion.

Preston Guardian 17th December 1853.

A story that is well documented occurred soon after the founding of the Institute for the Diffusion of Knowledge in 1828. In most town and cities, it would have been called the Mechanics' Institute, but it served the same purpose. Their first premises were on the eastern side of Cannon Street, and after moving equipment into the building, members were in attendance, sorting out books that had been gifted for the library. One of those involved was co-founder Joseph Livesey, better known for his temperance efforts. Time was getting late, and members were getting hungry and thirsty, so William Livesey, son of Joseph, was instructed to obtain ale and meat pies for their sustenance. The basketful of hot meat pies was obtained from a confectioner close to the Town Hall, and a big jug of ale was acquired at the Grey Horse. The pies apparently did not last long, but because many of the men rarely imbibed other than a cup of tea, the majority of the contents of the jug remained. This caused a little embarrassment to William who, of course, had to return the jug, but he found a solution "when he encountered a sturdy group of pilgrims of the night, who were engaged in their nocturnal vocation close by," and very willing to make it disappear! The quotation was not mine but adapted from a report made closer to the time of the event.

It is an interesting aside to look at the motives behind the Institute. It was an attempt to encourage workers to amend their drinking activities, with an ultimate aim of ceasing to drink alcohol permanently; but what were they to do to replace it? The answer was to educate them, and the 'Mechanics' Institute' was intended to do that. Subscription fees were set at 1s 7½d (8p) a quarter. The figure was based on a man depriving himself of thirteen 1½d glasses of ale each quarter. Just one glass each week. More wealthy members, which included those who founded the Institute were invited to pay what they could with no upper limit. Within months there were seven hundred members, and in 1850 the magnificent building that we later referred to as the Harris Art College opposite Avenham Colonnade, was opened as The Institute for the Diffusion of Knowledge. The University of Central Lancashire claim their heritage, and indeed, their foundation from the Institute.

Although better known in the later 19th and 20th century as Addisons', its name has always been the Grey Horse. Mary Addison married into the Yates's family, and wine bars were never the same again, later specialising in potent Australian white wines, a welcome compatriot on a cold day. For long enough it was, along with the Virgins' Inn in Anchor Weind, off the Market Place, the only thatched tavern in the town, but the Virgins' Inn went in the 1890's Town Improvements, and the Church Street inn was re-roofed in the 1930s. For a long time it remained one of the most frequented drinking holes in the town, despite the fact that it only had a six-day license, and for many years had closed on Sundays.

Its history can be traced back to at least 1808, but it was in about 1859 that Mary Addison became the landlord. In 1841 she was a twenty-three-year-old provision dealer with a three-year-old daughter, in the shop attached to and neighbouring the Grey Horse. In the late 1850s she acquired the license from her brothers, Peter, and Simon Yates, who were already involved in wholesaling as well as retailing wines and spirits. Mary was to develop her business along the same lines.

As long ago as the Court Leet Records of 1686, we see mention of a White Horse Inn, 'neare the Water Side'. Nothing is known, but a suggestion that it was by the River Ribble and close to where the Regatta Inn later appeared, may not be far from the mark. There have been suggestions that it was on the same site as, or possibly even the same building as the Regatta Inn.

During the 19th century, the White Horse Hotel on Friargate, at the point where it left Cheapside and the Market Place, was well known, but towards the end of that century the license was allowed to lapse, but it continued trading as a restaurant. There is evidence that it had existed since at least 1690, when it was in the control of Mrs. Sumner, and again in 1732 when it was run by Widow Phipps and owned by Widow Parkinson. Seemingly, when a lady lost her husband in those days, she instantly lost her personal identity. In 1796, Mrs. Palmer, also a widow following the death of Mr. Palmer, were the parents of Richard Palmer, the man who became Town Clerk for the town, serving fifty-one years in the role, as well as fifty-three years as a County Coroner; the years running concurrently. Richard was brought up at the White Horse, and Mrs. Palmer ran the business successfully for many years after her husband's death, but details are scant.

The much-recorded rebellion of 1745 had a significant impact on Preston, with several stories emanating from Friargate, from as far away as the corner of Back Lane where the Sun Hotel now stands, as far as this hotel. It is written that a man named Dickson, a sergeant in the rebel army, set out from the White Horse Hotel on a recruiting expedition to Manchester, accompanied by his mistress and a drummer. They marched throughout the night, and, arriving the following morning, immediately began to beat up for recruits for the "yellow-haired laddie." At first nobody bothered about his presence, but as the day wore on, a group formed around him with the intention of taking him prisoner. Dickson is reported to have presented his loaded blunderbuss and threatened to 'blow the brains out' of the first person to lay a hand on either him or his two close companions. Whilst the threat was hardly original in its content, it did have the effect of holding the mass at bay until assistance arrived in the form of a group of inhabitants of Manchester who were attached to the house of Stuart, and the opposition was successfully dispersed. He enlisted one hundred and eighty men who adopted the name, the Manchester Regiment.

You will, of course, have already read about the Black Horse Hotel on Friargate, about one hundred paces north of the White Horse.

Down by the Riverside

Above: Pleasure Boat Inn with workshop attached, left, the Bowling Green Inn, formerly the New Bridge Inn, with rounded boathouse attached to its eastern flank, and the Park Hotel standing aloft beyond the railway. The boathouse was later attached to the western side of the New Continental Hotel, illustrating exactly where the latter hotel was situated.

In an age when the most rapid mode of transport, other than the railway, was by horse, the footpath by the side of the River Ribble must have been a relaxing place to pass one's time.

The track, leading from the entrance to what is now Miller Park, to the point where it meets Broadgate, was bordered closely on one side by the river, and on the other side, for a part of its length, by a couple of hostelries, and a small number of dwellings, gardens, and plantsmen's nurseries, and referred to as Riverside or Ribbleside.

To recreate the picture from the third decade of the nineteenth century, we might start at what became the entrance to Miller Park by the North Union Railway bridge and begin our stroll downstream.

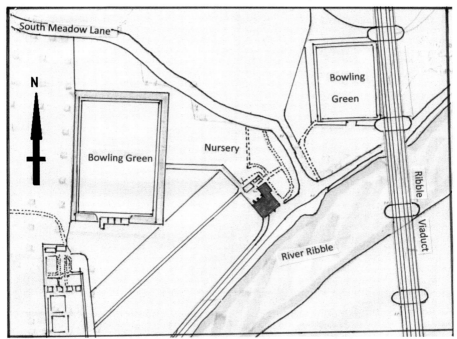

Above: The New Bridge Inn, later the Bowling Green Inn is marked red. The New Continental was built immediately to its right, and the Pleasure Boat Inn was built on the area that is clearly laid out as a (pleasure) gardens to the south of the bowling green, in the bottom left. South Meadow Lane was later straightened to meet the viaduct at its junction with Riverside.

The brackish waters that pass us at this point, are the waters that had recently begun to provide the baptismal waters for the recently arrived Mormons, who held their services along this stretch of the river from 1837 about one hundred and fifty yards upstream. The Old Continental Hotel is still about seventy years away from being built, but just yards beyond where it now stands, stood the Bowling Green Inn. It had previously been known as the New Bridge Inn, a nod to the new bridge that it had as a neighbour, the North Union Railway bridge, the viaduct which had been completed in about 1838.

The first date I have for the inn is 1837, when in September the premises were offered for tenancy by Charles Jackson, nurseryman, on whose land it stood. To the rear of the premises was a huge bowling green, that will now be just a portion of BAe's cricket pitch and sports area off South Meadow Lane. The land will have been a part of the garden nurseries that extended into what we now call Miller Park, and previously known as Avenham Gardens. The North Union Railway Company had acquired the land to build the new railway bridge across the river, which must prompt the question, 'Was the New Bridge Inn built by the railway company?' Although applications for the tenancy of the inn were to be addressed to Mr. C. Jackson, he may have been acting as an agent for the railway company having sold the property to them.

It will be seen on a map that two bowling greens were in existence at the rear, when the premises were still known as the New Bridge Inn, and evidence of a bowling match came in July 1851, when the landlord, William Dent, promoted a competition for thirty-two competitors, each of whom were to subscribe £1 to enter the sweepstake competition. The event was advertised as taking place 'at Dent's beautiful pleasure grounds, when there will be an attendance of the Blackburn Hand Bell Ringers', whose home was the Station Inn, Blackburn, and consisted of fourteen individual bellringers, with fifty-two bells between them, playing a selection of sacred music. In all, they appeared in the gardens on six separate dates, including the day of the bowling sweepstake, and dates both before and after it.

'Pleasure Gardens' were something that sprang up during the 18th and 19th centuries and needed to be little more than a garden to which the public were admitted for the purpose of recreation and entertainment, and it is believed that the **Pleasure Boat Inn** was built on the land marked clearly as (pleasure) gardens in about 1859. In 1907, when the inn was advertised for sale, there was mention of the land totalling 12,600 square yards, one composite of which could be

126 yards X 100 yards, so a substantially large area of land for such a purpose.

There had been earlier, but less notable bowling matches. In September 1846, sixteen entrants competed for a silver cup and a silver snuff box, followed by a dinner and entertainment, and exactly twelve months earlier, thirty members sat down to a celebratory meal, on the 5th Anniversary of the opening of the bowling green, thereby establishing the date for the creation of the green at soon after the inn first opened.

When the house was named the New Bridge Inn, it would be to differentiate it from the Bridge Inn on the other side of the river on Leyland Road. I first found it described as such in an October 1837 press notice, when it referred to an assignment of the assets of the tenant, Ann Wilkinson, which would suggest that she had been there for a period before that date, but it may not have been a long period. By December of that year she had left, and a further notice explaining how her debts would be paid appeared in the local paper.

Fifty yards further downstream we arrive at the Pleasure Boat Inn, but immediately before it we see a large, double-storey workshop to the right of it. The name, 'John Crook' could be seen in several places on boards around the assortment of buildings. These buildings, including some modifications to them, were used for many years, and known as 'The Mini-Centre,' a car service facility that originally catered only for the ever-popular mini motor car. Later they began servicing all makes of vehicle, and today, the inn is converted into two cottages.

John Crook, and his son, also John, were both boat-builders. In addition to that, the elder John ran the Pleasure Boat Inn with his wife Margaret. Another family which was linked with both the Pleasure Boat Inn and the Bowling Green Inn, were the Monks family, and it will be useful to know that Margaret Crook, prior to her marriage, had been Margaret Monk.

Above: The workshop to the right of the inn, was succeeded by the Mini Centre around fifty years ago.

In addition to boatbuilding and the pub trade, they also conducted a successful boat-hire business. Indeed, the occupants of both these inns conducted such a business, and on occasions, despite the family link, or maybe because of it, it created a great deal of friction between them.

The same was true about the Bowling Green inn, where both John Crook senior, and junior, had spells as licensee of that inn, but they could have been 'holding the fort' between permanent landlords.

In 1885, William Monk, a Preston man by birth, returned to the town after a lengthy spell in Canada, where four of his six children were born, and took over the Bowling Green Inn. He remained until 1894, when William Crook succeeded him there.

William was John junior's brother, and also a boat-builder. An example of how these two families worked together for their common good can be seen in 1860. Although John Crook senior appears in four consecutive Censuses from 1861, in 1870, William Monk held the licence of the Pleasure Boat Inn for several months before departing for Canada. What that allowed John senior to do, is not known, but it possibly gave him the opportunity to build the boats that he was to hire for use on the river in the summer months.

Unsurprisingly, where there are rowing boats and a tidal river, there will also be accidents, calamities, tragedies, and loss of life, but at the same time there can be displays of great heroism. There was never a shortage of any of those. It must be remembered that the river is tidal to a point far upstream, possibly another mile and a half to Brockholes, so an ebbing tide can be a dangerous foe.

Fortunately, John Crook senior was a man of extreme courage, and ever willing to put his own life in peril by rescuing those in difficulties, and there are records that prior to 1873, he had already saved the lives of twenty-three individuals! Embarrassingly, it was our neighbours in Blackburn who gave him the recognition he deserved, following an incident in April 1873 that involved two boys and two girls from that town. They had been harassed and eventually tipped out of their boat into the river, by several youths who were having a 'lark,' and John Crook was instrumental in saving them all. Ten years earlier, John Crook had saved the son of a former Superintendent of Police in Blackburn, and the two incidents had contributed to their council's action. When the news arrived that a presentation was to be made by the Blackburn Corporation, their Preston counterparts offered the use of our Town Hall for the ceremony. On the basis that all the money raised had been from sources in Blackburn, the offer was turned down, and it went ahead in the Ivy Inn, Infirmary Street, Blackburn, where he was presented with a framed testimonial, and a silver medal. Mrs. Crook was presented with a china tea service, 'as a slight acknowledgement of her exertions in resuscitating the sufferers her husband had saved.'

Left: The obverse side of the medal, making mention of the 23 lives saved to that date.

Below: The medallion with which John Crook was presented by the Humane Society.

The Pleasure Boat Inn hit the headlines on several occasions from around 1850, often following extremes in the weather, when the land extending out of the river became seriously flooded. In 1866, the cellars of the Pleasure Boat Inn were severely affected, with reports of the contents of them such as barrels of beer, wine and other floatable consumables being discovered far downstream, days after the events. Rescue attempts, often successful, were again carried out by John Crook, regardless of the cause. On this occasion, Mr Crook was praised for having saved a flock of forty sheep from peril and he gave an account of how he had, despite being a strong swimmer, almost lost his life when an embankment slipped and upset his boat, leaving him to swim against a torrent of water.

The nature of the area often attracted leisure pursuits other than boating, and one such event was planned for August 1864. A tight-rope walker called 'Signor Clare Duvalli'[1] had planned to erect a rope across the River Ribble, and walk across it, unaided, blind-folded, and in a sack, taking his dinner when he reached the centre of the rope!' Unfortunately, the previous week the Signor had almost fallen from his rope when trying to walk from the stage to the balcony in the Theatre Royal, Chester, and the magistrates and police called for the cancellation of the event, and despite huge gatherings on the riverbanks at the expected time, and with Signor Duvalli mingling among the crowds, the police were present to prevent any attempts to stage it.

In the same way that the Pleasure Boat Inn later had several revenue sources, such had been the case at the New Bridge Inn, with William Dent being a well-known florist, and who, at the height of his horticultural prowess, possessed a strip of land 'on the south side of Avenham' measuring just 25 yards by 16 yards, where he grew flowers that had gained him 'several hundred prizes.' He also ran a retail concern where he sold all manner of plants, from evergreens and shrubs to roses and azaleas and hardy border plants, plus fruit plants. Whether any of this land was part of that owned or run by Charles Jackson is not known, but it is highly likely.

When bowling contests were held, there was mention of the 'Pleasure Gardens' which surrounded the inn, but whether he grew

[1] *In 1859, Clare Duvalli traversed the River Tyne at Newcastle, crossing from the Gateshead side to Newcastle. It was said that 'he was a man of fifty-five summers, of little stature, and bearing traces of poverty. There was an immense crowd in attendance, but a collection carried out among them for his benefit, raised less than £1.*

anything in those gardens for his own purpose I do not know, but once again, it must be highly likely. In 1839, before he took the inn as landlord, there was a Dahlia Show presented here by the Ribblesdale Botanical Society, and there is no doubt that Dent would be a member of them, and he was certainly one of the exhibitors. The most prolific exhibitor, with many entries, was Daniel Whittle, who was gardener to Mrs. Ellen Cross at Red Scar, Grimsargh, who was the widow of Major William Cross. A complete list of the named varieties of Dahlias exhibited were given in the Preston Chronicle, which I am sure would be of great interest to gardeners and plantsmen of today as to whether any of the species still exist.

I do wonder whether the later inn, opened around 1859, took its inspiration from those 'pleasure gardens' to be named the Pleasure Boat Inn, for it was almost certainly occupying land, which was on part of, or adjacent to, those gardens.

A logical interest for a landlord whose inn ran by a major river, and particularly one so involved in many ways with that waterway, would be the product of it. I have come across a few instances where sea and river life has been displayed in public houses, with the prime intention of attracting custom. Early March in 1862 saw a large porpoise high up the river, arriving on a strongly running tide, and John Crook and others set off in pursuit of it. After what was described as 'some famous sport,' the creature had been peppered with so much shot that they were able to catch it and return with it to the Pleasure Boat Inn. It was there displayed for the benefit of their customers and others who had been attracted by his advertisement, "Extraordinary: NOW ON VIEW – JOHN CROOK'S "Pleasure Boat Inn," A LARGE PORPOISE PIG, caught in the Ribble. ADMISSION 1d. In 1883 John Crook Junior caught another porpoise, close to the Pleasure Boat Inn, and although they were common in the river, particularly around the estuary, it was rare for them to be seen so high upstream. On this occasion, however, it was displayed in a fishmonger's window in the town centre. It measured 5 feet (1.5 metres) in length and weighed two hundredweight.

A similar outcome followed the pursuit by three boats of a large sturgeon up the river towards Walton Deeps and the bridge over London Road in June 1870. They were being encouraged in their pursuit by Mr. Ware, a fishmonger in Preston. The fish survived several gunshot wounds and pitchfork attacks but was eventually caught by a rope around its tail and hauled to the bank. Although John Crook had played no part in the catching of the fish, it was on display in the Pleasure Boat Inn the following day. It was described as 8 feet 1 inch (over 2 metres) in length, 3 feet 2 inches (just less than one metre) around its girth, and weighed 183 lbs.

In 1864, following the death of its owner, John Crook had acquired, certainly for the duration of his purposes, a large collection of glass-cased British and Foreign Birds, including a colossal Emu, a Bewick Swan, a Bittern, and several Birds of Paradise. The following year, at the Preston Exhibition, John Crook displayed a beautiful model of a barque, and a model of a schooner, made from the breastbone of a bantam cock.

Prior to the arrival of the Crooks and the Monks, I have seen no reference to commercial pleasure boating, and for many years their respective businesses were generally conducted in an uneventful fashion. However, the summer of 1887 was to be a season of friction between the related but competing families, as they fought (sometimes literally) for the boat trade that was on offer.

Mrs. Martha Monk, the wife of William Monk, the landlord of the Bowling Green Inn, took great objection to a man named John Ellison, a labourer employed by John Crook, who was walking past Monk's inn with a group of men who wanted to hire a boat to sail. Without any provocation, Martha approached Ellison and punched him in the face. The resultant court case was dismissed on condition that Mrs. Monk paid the costs of the case. Having seen many such cases and similar outcomes, it was the Victorian way of implying that it was a case of six of one and half a dozen of the other, with the full details never being known outside of the two protagonists.

What is known, is that just two days later, the acrimony resurfaced. This time the row was between two of the sons, William Crook and Henry Monk, with the former making an allegation of assault against the other. On this occasion, William told the court that he had been standing on the landing stage with two gentlemen, talking to them about selling them some boats, when Henry's father came down the river in a boat and called out to the men, "If you want cheap boats, come to my place." Miss. Crook, one of John's daughters, then asked him if he had finished, and requested him to send down the 'spy.'

Mr. Monk senior then came down to the river, asking who had called him a spy, and the complainant said, "All of us!" The defendant said, "Come up; I'll settle with you first." The complainant said that he went up the steps, and when he was a couple of steps from the top, the defendant struck him on the neck. As he fell backwards, he caught hold of a stanchion, or he would certainly have fallen to the bottom. Henry Monk was convicted and fined ten shillings plus the costs of the case, or in default of that, to be imprisoned for seven days.

Such can be the life of families when they are neighbours as well as competitors.

Having recounted the heroism of John Crook Senior, and the accidents that had led to those acts, I feel a need to add a tale of caution of the ever-present dangers of any sort of water body, let alone a major tidal river. The story began in early September 1902, at the home of John Crook Junior, who was, by this time living at an address in Euston Street in the Fishergate Hill area. John Junior's son, Thomas Crook, aged 11 years, went to the house of one of his neighbours for the purpose of taking their son, John Arkwright Ashcroft, aged 3 years 9 months, for a ride in a handcart. It was something that he did regularly, and on this occasion took him to John's boatyard at the Pleasure Boat Inn. The boy's mother gave Thomas a penny and made him promise that he would not take the child in a boat on the river.

However, once down by the river, the child began crying to be taken on a boat, so Thomas asked his 14-year-old brother Ernest for permission to do so, but he refused to allow him. The child continued to cry, so Thomas took a boat secretively, and took both the child and another boy onto the river. As could be predicted, the child asked several times during the sail to be moved to a different part of the boat, and on one of those occasions, Thomas lost his footing, and both he and the young child fell overboard. The remaining boy used an oar to save Thomas, but the child was never seen again until he was later taken from the water using grappling irons. I feel sure that the irony of this incident was not lost on John Crook Senior, who by this time was 70 years of age.

Nevertheless, tragedy was to strike again just two months later, when the landlord was John Atkinson. He had taken over the inn in 1899, but John Crook Junior still built boats in the boathouse adjacent. In December 1902, the river was extremely full, there having been a lot of recent rainfall. Coupled with that there was a strong, ebbing tide. Many of the rowing boats tied up on the south side of the river were in danger of being washed away, so John Atkinson and his 13-year-old son, Robert, went across to the other side of the river for the purpose of moving the boats to safety.

They brought the first boat across the strongly flowing river, but as they were attempting to tie it up to boats that were already moored, their boat turned broadside to the flow and was instantly overturned. They were both thrown into the river, but John managed to keep hold of his son, telling him to climb onto his back. He then leapt for an anchoring chain and the boy became dislodged and washed away. It was later seen as perversely fortunate that the boy had disappeared completely from view, for if he had been visible the father is almost certain to have attempted to rescue him. The state and condition of the river at the time would have meant almost certain death for both. Alas, the whole tragedy was witnessed by John's wife and the child's mother, Margaret, from an upstairs bedroom window of the inn, unable to assist in any way, and presumably consumed by fear and despair.

As I have already mentioned, 1907 saw the Bowling Green Inn being advertised for sale, and it was then that Thomas Croft, one of Preston's better-known builders at the time was the buyer of it. What his intentions were will never be known in detail, but between then and 1911 when he built and opened what was originally known as the Old Continental Hotel, a series of events occurred that may or may not have been anticipated.

Included in his building plans were about six houses at the end of South Meadow Lane, closest to Miller Park, and overlooking the cricket ground. All of those and the Continental itself, were flat-roofed. They were cheaper to build without a pitched roof, and that money-saving feature suited Tom Croft. It is said that when he built an office at his brickworks in Ribbleton, he instructed the bricklayers to lay the bricks on edge, rather than in the conventional manner, because they would use less bricks!

From the outset, the aim was to provide premises, a home and a living for his daughter and son-in-law, Samuel Thomson. Sammy Thomson was a key member of the 1888 Preston North End 'Invincibles', the team that won the football league of that year without losing a game, and the F.A. Cup without conceding a goal. He was a well-known figure locally, and a priceless attraction to a venue such as the one Croft envisaged. Thomson spent some time as licensee of the Bowling Green Inn whilst the Continental was being built, and when complete, he moved next door, and the Bowling Green Inn was demolished.

When the licence for the Continental was first applied for, it was stipulated that the Pleasure Boat Inn, which Croft had also bought, should forfeit its licence, which was something that Croft readily agreed to. Whether he had alternative plans for the Pleasure Boat Inn if that stipulation had not been introduced is not known, but in view of the fact that he had not voluntarily put that intention forward perhaps suggests that he had.

Returning to the demolition of the Bowling Green Inn, the one part of it that remained was the Boat House, that had amusingly, in the 1907 sale advertisement, been referred to as a 'Bowl-House.' Whether the clerk at the Lancashire Evening Post had misheard 'Boat' for 'Bowl,' or misread a written instruction is not clear, but perhaps it is understandable, based on the name of the inn.

Wherever the misunderstanding lay, the original Boat House, on the east of the Bowling Green Inn, became the Boat House on the west of the Old Continental Hotel, a fact that implies that pleasure-boat hire was going to continue, and now unhindered by opposition from its neighbours. It did.

The Old Continental Hotel has, during the last one hundred years, undergone many works of modernisation, including the removal of the Boat House, and now flourishes as the New Continental Hotel and Beer Gardens, in its enviable position by the river.

NEW COCK INN

New Cock Yard, Fishergate

Before beginning to consider the history of the New Cock Inn, it is necessary to reflect on a much more distant period when Preston, before the advent of the cotton industry, was a residential town, and the townhouses of the wealthy on the main thoroughfares had impressive gardens. Some of those on the southern side of Fishergate ran as far back as Cross Street, a distance of some 150 metres. Several of these townhouses were later converted into inns and taverns. For example, the Castle Inn on Cheapside was once the home of the Rawsthorne family, of Hutton, and the Cross Keys Inn, opposite the Castle Inn in the northeast corner of the Market Place, was the residence of the Duke of Hamilton.

In the case of the New Cock, it was at one time the home of Thomas Winckley, the last male descendant of the Winckley family of Preston, and the father of Lady Frances Shelley. The family owned vast swathes of land in Preston, and Winckley Square is sited on just a part of it. He did not spend a great deal of time in Preston, preferring the high life with his aristocratic friends in London. It was said that long after his death in 1794, his conversational charm and wit was well remembered.

A wonderful story persists around why Thomas Winckley decided to leave Preston altogether, and perhaps illustrated the transitional period into the industrial revolution, which in Preston was principally the cotton industry. Thomas had visited a fishmonger in the town, and noticing a very fine turbot, he ordered that it should be sent to his house. He was told by the shopkeeper that it was already sold, and he learned that the purchaser was John Horrocks, the young cotton manufacturer, Winckley, who apparently had a violent temper, declared that Preston was no longer a place for the gentry, and almost immediately left his house and never returned. This was around 1793; and within a couple of years, Winckley House was partially demolished, and the rear portion became the New Cock Inn.

Originally, an ancient signboard was displayed at the entrance to New Cock Yard from its opening on Fishergate. It displayed a young cock in full colour. With flowing tail and its head held proudly erect, its comb and ears both bright red, and with its beak wide apart as if in the act of crowing.

It is not known why the inn was given its name, but I doubt that when, in the 6th century, Pope Gregory the First declared the cock to be the most suitable emblem of Christianity, that he had such a use in mind. At the time it first opened, cockfighting was still a well-practiced sport in the town, deemed by many to be just another form of gambling, and carried out in several parts of the town, including the Derby's Cockpit behind what is now the Minster. That there was a cockpit inside the New Cock Inn is less known, but when it was demolished in the late 1970s, it was found that the cockpit was still there, on the upper floor, and a number of local historians took advantage to inspect it. It was described as being set deep beneath a surrounding timber balustrade. Around the same time a descendant of Joseph Wilson, landlord of the inn from 1921 until 1931 added that she had learned anecdotally that not only did cockfighting take place on the premises, but dogfighting was also conducted in the yard, all for the benefit of those who wished to gamble on the various outcomes.

Joseph Wilson could have been speaking words of gambling experience, for in May 1931, the year his tenure came to an end, he was entertaining a number of his friends who were visiting from Darwen. In the early hours one Saturday morning, a passing policeman heard voices coming from the first-floor kitchen of the New Cock Inn. The lights were on, and the blinds were not drawn. He found and mounted a ladder and looking over the frosted portion of the window discovered that Wilson, along with his friends were sitting round a table playing cards. Various amounts of money were on the table in front of each participant, with Wilson, who was 'banker' at the time having the largest amount. He was heard to say, "Come on lads, get your money on," and the policeman saw stakes of between ten shillings and fifty shillings being placed.

Along with other officers, the police entered the public house, gaining access through the unlocked front entrance, and made their way to the kitchen, where they found Wilson with a bundle of notes in his hand. He was told he would be reported for permitting gambling on licensed premises but replied that he would gamble as much as he like in his own private quarters. Unfortunately, he was to discover that his license extended to all parts of his premises, including the private quarters, but the magistrates took the view that although a licensee's home, unlike those of other Englishmen, is not also his castle, they felt that justice would be served if Wilson paid the costs of the case. It was, nevertheless, a salutary lesson for other licensees in the town.

A long-serving licensee, Dick Sumner, and his wife, who were there from 1952 until 1966, told the tale that following a fire in the living quarters, the brewery rebuilt most of the house, and at the same time 'the cock-pit was lopped off.' Perhaps sealed off was a more accurate description because it was re-discovered in 1978 as I have already mentioned. Indeed, it has been said that the Derby-owned Derby Arms that stood at one time on Back Lane, now Market Street, and previously known as the Cock and Bottle, made use of the nearby cockpit in Starch-house Square. On Lang's map of Preston, dated 1774, there was an oblong enclosure marked at the southern end of what it now Adelphi Street and the Adelphi Hotel. Indeed, although there was a replacement Fighting Cocks Tavern on Fylde Street at the end of Friargate, it is believed that the original one stood on the same site as the present Adelphi Hotel, and close to the enclosure to which I have just referred, all serving to indicate how prevalent cockfighting was in Preston. In fact, as late as 1862, the landlord at the Sir Walter Scott on North Road, and again in 1870 the landlord of the Bee Hive Inn in Marsh Lane were prosecuted for allowing cockfighting on their premises.

The New Cock Inn, when it existed, was probably the oldest building in Preston, and an example of a townhouse, or at least part of one, being altered to an inn. Certainly in 1941, there was, on the inside of the entrance door in New Cock Yard, the date 1612, scratched with a sharp implement. The premises were previously the servant's quarters of the Winckley mansion, and the three shops in Fishergate immediately to the right of New Cock Yard as you entered it from Fishergate, occupy the area that was once the mansion. The whole is now consumed by Boots the Chemists.

It is recorded that as late as 1880, there was a wooden beam over the entrance showing the date 1625, but that had been replaced by an iron girder.

The first recorded licensee of the inn was William Ascroft, whose name occurs on a Polling list of 1812, and whose home-brewed ale gained high acclaim. He was the father of Robert Ascroft, who for almost a quarter of a century was the Town Clerk of Preston, and it was Robert who founded the firm of solicitors R. & W. Ascroft, and who had their first offices in New Cock Yard.

Whether Ascroft was the first landlord, or whether the birth of it was prior to 1812 is not known. From the demolishing of the house in about 1795 there are some seventeen years unaccounted for.

Other licensees were mentioned from 1829, but in 1833 Ascroft is advertising the inn to let, together with the brewhouse, and stabling for 30 to 40 horses. The New Cock was never a major coaching inn, but in 1833, an advertisement appeared for a new 'LIGHT POST COACH,' which was to run from the neighbouring Old Legs of Man Coach Office, and the New Cock Inn to the Hesketh Arms in Southport three days a week, and on Saturday to Leeds, Rochdale, and Halifax. By early 1835, accommodation was being offered to travellers.

In that year, the New Cock was tenanted by Samuel Wood. The first couple of years of his tenancy were unexceptional, but in 1835, he became embroiled in the election riots of that year that earned it a place in Hansard in May of that year. The entry in that book of Parliamentary debates, used words like bribery, outrage and violence, the use of wealth to seduce, and the use of power to coerce. It linked the two together to indicate how the combination of coercion and seduction were used to obstruct the conscientious voter. The two political parties involved following the decision that Radical Henry 'The Orator' Hunt had taken not to run for office, were the Conservatives and the Whigs. The Radicals who had followed Hunt, had formed an alliance with the Whigs.

The main headquarters of the Conservatives was at the Albion Hotel, later to be known as the Royal Hotel in Church Street. It stood, as we will rediscover in the next chapter, immediately across the road from the Old Dog Inn. They also used a room for their meetings in a place in Pole Street known by the name of the Clock Face Tavern. Those two places, on separate occasions were targeted by the opposing political factions; and such was the damage caused at the Albion, it was known for a time as The Glass Barrel Hotel. Very little imagination needs to be used.

Staying with Samuel Woods for a while, it was alleged that on the 13th of January 1835, Samuel Wood struck a man at the bottom of New Cock Yard with a stick, without any provocation, and broke the man's arm. He further was accused of kicking and threatening to kill him. It was said in the report that the yard was a regular rendez-vous for the Blues, whereas the New Cock Inn and its clientele were affiliated to the opposing party of Whigs. He was committed to the Sessions to answer the charge, but no record has been found of the outcome.

Whether the above attack had any bearing on what happened five days earlier I do not know, but on the 8th of January, there took place the series of incidents to which a Hansard entry referred in particular. At the Assizes in Lancaster in August of the same year, a special constable gave evidence to say that he knew Samuel Woods very well, and that he knew him to be the landlord of the Fighting Cocks. Now that was a common ploy to avoid a particular tavern getting a poor reputation, but I am certain that he was the landlord of the New Cock Inn. Ironically, and possibly a reason for the mistake, was that the Fighting Cocks Tavern, which stood where the Adelphi Hotel now stands, was also involved in the election riots. The constable said that on the day in question, 'Woods' house was full of bludgeon-men, and that they had plentiful supplies of beer, and were ladling it out from buckets.' He had heard Woods say to the men that they could not stop there, 'but must go and have another row.' He had continued by saying, 'We must fetch these devils out of the Albion, or we must pull the house down.' It appears that the witness had visited the house with a regular constable, but whether it was the distance he was from people or the general noise in the place, the latter seemed not to have heard all that the special constable had heard.

On reaching the Clockface Tavern, so called because it displayed on an exterior wall, a false clock with artificial fingers, in place of a more usual pub sign, the landlady said that the mob broke open the locked and barred door, and that the men were armed with bludgeons and sticks. The windows were guarded by shutters that were fastened on the inside. Men came in by both the front and rear entrances, knocked canisters off the shelves, and strewed the goods about. A man went to the woman and demanded, "Damned you, where are the colours?" She told him that there were no colours in the house. Stones were then thrown and all the windows in the house were shattered, and the frames destroyed as well.

A witness reported that between three and four o'clock in the afternoon, he had seen a crowd approaching the Clockface. He said that Samuel Woods was leading the men. On reaching the tavern, the door was broken open, and the witness said that Woods stood on the top of the steps into the tavern and said to the men in a loud voice, "Now lads, do your duty." The fingers of the clock were torn down and in a short while the windows were smashed. The witness said that he had first seen Woods, "near the chapel". Carey Baptist Church, which was built in 1826, but known at that time as St. Paul's Chapel, is most likely the chapel being referred to, which would suggest that the Clockface Tavern was north of Percy Street and Lord's Walk.

A further witness told the Court that he was near the Clockface Tavern, and within a yard or two of Woods, when he heard him say, "Now my lads, you've done enough, go away; the constables are coming."

In defence of Woods, one Dr. Brown made great play of the certainty of witnesses giving false information in order to gain a conviction in the case of election riots, and he added that there would be no lack of zeal in their prosecution, for attorneys were very willing to take up the cases, in the knowledge that the country would have to pay the costs. I have my doubts as to whether Dr. Brown was a lawyer, for he had a lot to say about the delaying tactics of the attorneys which he considered disadvantageous to Woods, saying, "Such conduct is not honourable, however convenient it might be."

Dr. Brown said that he felt considerable anxiety on the part of his client, on account of the respectability of his station in life, being a master stonemason, and the difficulty of proving in August what had happened in January. Despite that, he then called a series of witnesses to say that Woods was in his own house from around mid-day on the day in question, after his own house, the New Cock Inn, had been attacked, and all the windows broken. The 'red caps' had gone away at about one o'clock, and the police were being awaited. He went on to say that Woods was in the bar from one o'clock until six or seven at night, filling liquor and ale, because the house was full, but he saw no bludgeons.

In fact, a series of witnesses were brought to say that they had seen no bludgeons, before he called a witness who had been at the Clockface Tavern, who was adamant that Woods was not present there. The witness's occupation? He was a master stonemason!

Despite the fact that Dr. Brown failed to re-mention that untruths could be expected in cases of election rioting, he did sufficient to induce the jury of twelve good men and true, to find him innocent.

Despite that, after the January 17th assault on the man in New Cock Yard by Woods, he left the inn, and by the 14th of February, the next landlord had moved in, and was advertising his arrival, and life returned to some sort of normality.

The Albion Hotel

Later known as the Imperial Hotel and the Royal Hotel

Church Street

STORIES OF DAMAGE AND DEBAUCHERY

Many of the tales about Preston's licensed past could possibly be labelled 'murky,' but it is debatable whether we can plumb depths much lower than this one! That is quite a paradox, because prior to its arrival as a public house in about 1832, it had been the home of the Grimshaw family as well as Thomas Batty Addison, a lawyer, and renowned Recorder of Preston.

During its licensed life it acquired an assortment of names, some intended to avoid damaging the poor reputation likely to be gained after an unsavoury occurrence, including one which was descriptive of its poor reputation, but before going any further, let me explain where the Albion Hotel stood.

Left: The Albion was immediately across the road from the entrance to St. John's Place, next to the Minster. In the photograph I can imagine myself standing in that position to admire the Preston Guild decorations on the front face of the hotel in 1902, by which time it was known as the Royal Hotel. At other periods in its existence, it was known as the Imperial Hotel between 1857 and 1860, and for a couple of years around 1881 as the Glass Barrel Hotel, for in disturbances there was always an abundance of broken beer glasses or windows, and its reputation during election riots.

In an 1881 court case, it was once again described as the Glass Barrel Hotel, and given to the court as that. Whether it recalled the election riots of the 1830s, or whether there had been a glut of recent incidents is not clear, but one person was fined for such behaviour. Mary Cogan was prosecuted for causing damage to the value of 3s 8d, and from the little bit I know about her, I can tell you she was a prostitute who had a connection to Blelock Street, off Shepherd Street, in the infamous Sandhole area of the town, and she was in the habit of 'entertaining soldiers.' I can further tell you that if you see 'Blelock Street' and 'soldiers' in the same sentence, the only word missing is 'prostitute.' In 1879, it was said that Mary Cogan had been before the court on twenty-three previous occasions, although to be fair, they were not all for prostitution.

On the current occasion, by which time she had reached her thirtieth return to the court, the case was proved by P.C. Ash, and she was fined 2s 6d (12½p), told to pay the costs of the damage, or if she failed, to spend seven days in prison.

Whilst speaking of damage in public houses, the Albion suffered more than many during the period of elections, and 'election sports,' as they were called, seemed to require as much damage being inflicted as possible. The Albion was the headquarters for one political party, and therefore deemed to be fair game by the opposition. During one spell of electioneering sports, 'everything that was breakable in this establishment, was broken.'

During the elections of 1835, as we have already seen, there was some mischief that had its origins in the New Cock Inn on Fishergate, as we saw in the last chapter

At about 7 o'clock one evening, a numerous body of men went to the Albion, and commenced an attack on it using bludgeons, iron bars, and other weapons. The door was closed when they arrived, but they broke in and destroyed everything that lay within their reach, from the furniture to the windows and doors. They went even further, by ransacking the drawers of the fixtures, and threw the whole of the combustible articles they found in them onto the fire in the bar.

While the work of destruction was going on, the Chief Constable, with about eighty Special Constables, arrived at the Albion, and by persuasion, and the sizeable appearance of the force he had brought with him, succeeded in inducing them to desist.

A mechanic, who lived in High Street, said in court, that he had been standing outside the Grey Horse public house in Church Street, at the material time, when he saw several men come out of the inn, meeting with others who were already outside. He distinctly heard it said that "We'll go and pull down the Albion and destroy it. Some were wearing bonnets, blue and yellow mixed together, and they later came back with some red bonnets."

Returning to the photograph for a moment, try to imagine the view through the broad coach entrance or passageway that is just visible on the right-hand side of the hotel. Through it you would have entered a cobbled yard. On the right-hand side of the yard was the entrance to what was, in around 1850, a concert hall, and was, for many years later, a warehouse.

The Albion was almost certainly the first licensed premises in Preston to offer concert hall entertainment. Indeed, in the 1851 Census there were several young musicians recorded as staying there at the time. There had clearly been performances there for long enough for it to have acquired a reputation, for in 1850 at the latest, a report was compiled by someone said to be a Reverend gentleman, and another man connected to Preston Prison. They were Charles Castles and Amos Wilson.

Perhaps we can learn something from two items in the local newspapers in 1841. Firstly, in the April of that year, 'Anthropos' writes a letter to the editor which he publishes. It is headed 'Singing Rooms,' and is an appeal for the newspaper to take a lead in the exposing of the disadvantages of 'these dens of vice and pollution – the singing rooms and cheap concert halls'. In the November of the same year the Albion Hotel was advertised to be let. Among the accommodation described were two large concert rooms, both in excess of fifty feet in length, and both around thirty feet in width. In the space available between the hotel yard and neighbouring Clarke's Yard, a passageway from Church Street to Lord's Walk. I can say that the rooms ran in a line rather than parallel to one another, and there was a Tap Room attached to them. There was a Spirit Vault either in, or under, the hotel itself, and in the yard was a Brewhouse and stabling for fifteen horses.

In 1856 a similar advertisement appeared, and there was no mention of concert rooms or accommodation of a similar size. The problem had been quelled, or it had moved elsewhere.

I have found that Castles was more likely to have been a schoolteacher rather than a Reverend, a man who lived in Alfred Street, off Park Road. Amos Wilson, a turnkey at the prison, was a year older than Castles at 34 years and lived around 100 metres distant from him in Percy Street.

Both men had become alarmed at the potential evil encouraged to those attending the concerts and had published a report condemning them. Their report concentrated on 'the principal singing-room in the town and its effects on our society.' On one visit they describe what would seem to be the presentation of a stage play, followed by singing and dancing, with the evening concluding with a performance of 'The Spare Bed,' something which they understood to have been 'eagerly anticipated by the audience,' but described by them as 'an abominable piece.' It would appear to have involved a man getting undressed for bed, right down to the flesh-hugging, tight-fitting garment he was wearing underneath. All in all, the performance was 'suggestive and full of innuendoes.'

The authors of the report also gave a useful if graphic description of the premises. There were two prices of admission, and our moral guardians chose the 4d rather than the 2d entrance charge, because they 'were desirous of seeing as much as they could.' They went on to describe that when the performance began, 'and what with the mouthing of the performers, the vociferous shouts, the maledictions, the want of light, and the smoke from about a hundred clay pipes, the effect was bewildering for a few minutes.'

They described the hall as being capable of holding between 800 and 1,000 people. One end is fitted up with a stage, and the bar, where the liquors are served is placed in the middle. The place between the bar and the stage is appropriated to the juveniles, boys and girls from 10 to 14 years of age; of them there were not less than a hundred, and many of the boys were both drinking and smoking,

The area behind the bar would appear to have been fitted up for the 'respectable people' the seats being 'more commodious,' although they went on to report that during the whole evening (yes, our report writers stayed all evening), they did not see more than half a dozen respectable working men, but what constituted being respectable is not clear.

They went on to describe that, 'leaving this lower part of the room we had to proceed up a dark staircase, with some parts almost impassable because of the crowds of young people.'

To reach the top gallery 'we had to mount some more crazy stairs.' The upper gallery was composed of two short side-sittings, and four boxes in front. 'The occupants of these boxes are totally secluded from the eyes of the rest of the audience.' No matter where I have looked, I have found no clue as to who might have been among them!

Away from the dubious frivolities of the evening and night, I feel sure that during a normal working day, the rest of the premises took on a totally different appearance. A huge yard lay through the coach entrance and behind the hotel premises, and had, in one corner of the yard, a blacksmith's workshop, with the attendant toing and froing of tradesmen's horses and ponies being reshod. Yet the hotel never was noted as a coaching house.

In 1836, James Newsham became the landlord. He was also a coach proprietor, so perhaps he had thoughts of starting such a business from these premises. In 1837, an advertisement appeared offering Superior coach travel to Liverpool on the Rein Deer Coach, operated by five other people. The content of the notice seemed to imply that there was a cartel of coach proprietors in operation in Preston, and probably elsewhere, by saying that 'in spite of monopolizers' the Rein Deer Light Post Coach would run every morning at 6.30am from the Albion Hotel.

A more unusual venture that James Newsham was a party to, occurred soon after he took over at the Albion. It took the form of a trip to Chester Races by boat. It was promoted by Newsham and John Eamer, a porter dealer in St. John's Place. Custom was drawn from the Albion, as well as the Old Legs of Man opposite the old Town Hall, and the Corporation Arms in Lune Street. Newshams' responsibility lay in the transporting of the traveller's luggage, on the evening prior to sailing, to the bottom of Fishergate, where the Steamer, 'Enterprise' was moored at the New Quay. It set sail at 10am on Sunday 1st May and was due to call at Lytham and Southport to pick up further passengers, before arriving in Chester in the early evening. The return journey, including First Class accommodation was to cost less than £1 per person but I doubt if any of the protagonists in the election riots thirteen months earlier made the trip.

In 1838, Charles Worthington succeeded Newsham as landlord, but he only remained a few months, for on the 1st October of that year, he moved to the 'large and commodious' Victoria and Station Hotel, opposite the entrance to Butler Street, and is advertising all manner of services as a hotelier to families and commercial gentlemen, including stabling and facilities for coaches, but there was never any suggestion that he wished to conduct a regular coaching service either there or at the Albion. By 1840, he had been declared bankrupt.

Following the concert hall days of the 1840s and early 1850s, there was no further mention of entertainment at the Albion, the Imperial, or, indeed the Royal Hotel, until, in 1879, when a new landlord advertised in The Era, the entertainment newspaper, for a lady vocalist and a pianist to live on the premises. It was a fleeting enterprise, and whether there was a direct connection to those efforts being simultaneous with the time it was known as the Glass Barrel Hotel, is not known. By the time 1890 arrived, the courts were making efforts to reduce musical entertainment on licensed premises across Preston, by refusing to license them for such purposes.

A final throw of the dice was attempted in 1901 when the landlord became Robert Taylor. He began, almost immediately, to offer entertainment, but found himself summoned under the Preston Improvement Act 1889. Under that Act, entertainment of any description was outlawed, but in Taylor's case it made a particular point that he had employed professional entertainers.

The final years of the hotel were unremarkable, but in late 1911, the hotel was bought by the County Wine Stores who operated in the premises of the Old King's Head Inn at the corner of Bamber's Yard. For years the Royal Hotel and its predecessors had possessed wholesale wine and spirit vaults, and must have fitted their business needs perfectly. The hotel closed in 1915.

From the Garths Arms to the Rifleman

Avenham Street to Water Street

Left: The Garth's Arms, later the Duke of Windsor, seen here during its life as Gaston's Continental Bar.

The rear of the premises opened onto Old Cock Yard, a feature that presented a number of clientele problems in the 1800s.

Fathoming the truth, is one of the challenges, and yet at the same time, one of the joys in the struggle to unravel our local history. This is particularly so when primary source material is scant or absent, and sometimes conflicting secondary evidence is the only source available. Occasionally one must be satisfied that all the i's have not been dotted, and yet usually, it only marginally affects the overall story.

Such is the case with the Garth's Arms and the Rifleman Inn, two hostelries that in many ways could not be more different than chalk is to cheese, but as I will explain, they presented several conundrums. There was also the occasional similarity. To do so, I will need to introduce a third hostelry, the Black Bull Inn, often

129

referred to as 'The Bull,' which stood on Cheapside until 1861, and formed a portion of the complex that included the old Town Hall. The metal base of a pinioning ring can still be found in the Market Place, evidence of bullbaiting in years long forgotten. The Bull was one of many inns and taverns that regularly hosted bankruptcy hearings, and it was one such that played its part in one example of those confusions.

I need now to mention some names of significant players in the story; the Garth family, and the Ogles. With a name like Ogle, one would assume that the possibility of confusion would be low, but we have all heard about the dangers of assuming, and particularly in a case like this, where both men with the same surname, had been christened Thomas. Such was the case here. Indeed, I came across a third Thomas Ogle, a fraudster, who appeared at Clerkenwell Sessions House in December 1801. Like most swindlers, he had several aliases, including the impressive Surtees Pullen, but he was sentenced in that year to seven years transportation to the colonies, so I can safely eliminate him from consideration during the years I am interested in.

I had first encountered Admiral Thomas Ogle living at a house in Avenham Street, off Church Street, a much-decorated naval man who married Mary, the eldest daughter of John Garth. Garth was the landlord at the Black Bull Inn, Cheapside, from 1801 until 1809, and hosted several episodes of what appeared to be a turbulent first decade of bankruptcy hearings for the other Thomas Ogle. I suspect that this Thomas Ogle had an eclectic mixture of business interests, for in 1805, he dissolved a partnership with Francis Brackenbury and Robert Roper, with whom he had been a cotton manufacturer. Two years later, he dissolved a partnership he had had with two Blackburn gentlemen, Joseph Messenger, and Joseph Dutton, with whom he operated as a liquor merchant.

A lot of his business interests centred on the area on the south side of Church Street in Preston, stretching from Water Street (the lower length of what is now known as Manchester Road), to Dale Street, opposite the prison at the bottom of Church Street. His interests continued into properties in Leeming Street, the part of what is now Manchester Road from Shepherd Street to Queen Street and Avenham Lane. Beyond that it was known as King Street.

One of the properties with which Ogle, and his associates had an interest was the Rifleman Inn, premises that make their appearance at the beginning of the 1800s. A lot of the property in the area was, as I have already indicated, in common ownership, and the occupiers of the neighbouring stables and warehouses to the Rifleman, were Thomas Ogle and Samuel Horrocks Junior. In 1803, both Ogle and Horrocks were volunteers with Royal Lancashire Regiment of Militia, with Ogle described as Captain Thomas Ogle, and Horrocks Junior as his 2nd Lieutenant in the same Company. The name of the Company? It was the Rifle Company, and that, for most people, including me, would be sufficient to explain the origin of the inn's name.

It may have been a surprise that the two establishments we are considering had some similarities. It involved the clientele that frequented the houses in both instances, but in the case of the Rifleman it may be less of a surprise that in addition to the thieves and vagabonds, they also had an attraction for the other scourge, prostitutes, living predominantly to the rear of the house in the Sandhole area, adjacent to Shepherd Street. One could not sink lower than live in the Sandhole, and their residence in the cellars of those basic dwellings attracted soldiers, the occasional sailor, and members of the militia to the area, and to this, as well as other neighbouring taverns. Skirmishes of all description were common-place, and unsuspecting, or more likely naïve country folk who were visiting town to meet some of the ladies, were very often relieved of more cash than they had budgeted for.

A good example of such a theft happened in 1871, when a man, a reed-maker by trade, from Ramsbottom, came to the town, and having arrived in the Sandhole district, engaged in conversation with a man who was sitting on his doorstep in Shepherd Street. After some time, they decided that a glass of ale in the White Lion at the end of the street would be the order of the day, and whilst there, our man from the east of the county, was introduced to three young ladies. The young ladies, no doubt having the ability to sniff out an opportunity when presented with one, spent considerable time and effort in ensuring that their potential victim consumed sufficient ale, together with the odd glass of rum, in order to affect his judgement.

A point arrived when they considered him to be at the stage where they might induce him to accompany them to their own territory, namely the Rifleman Inn. Once there, their operations began in earnest. He had arrived in Preston with eleven half sovereigns, and seven shillings in silver. He departed with nothing. They also relieved him of his best pocket handkerchief, a commonly stolen item which would be pawned the following day.

Around 1870, the judiciary made a concerted effort to make the landlords of licensed premises responsible for who they allowed to resort in their premises. It was an almost impossible position for them, for while they may know the courtroom history of some of their clientele, it was deemed an unreasonable expectation that they would have an extensive knowledge. Furthermore, there was a counter view that even thieves and prostitutes should be allowed to avail themselves of the refreshments available in the inns, and for how long they should be allowed to remain on or within the premises.

The Garth's Arms on the other hand, stood across the road from the old police station in Avenham Street and Turk's Head Yard, and should, in theory have presented a lesser problem. The problem would appear to be that there was also a rear entrance to the tavern from Old Cock Yard, and although the property there was marginally superior to the Sandhole, it was not by a significant amount, and many were occupied by ladies of the night, able to access the haunt of better class gentlemen and others. There was a room on the first floor for discerning gentlemen to meet, as well as to avoid more the fundamental business being conducted at times on the ground floor. Most importantly, poor publicity regarding this type of clientele would appear to have been avoided.

The Avenham Street house that had been the possession of Thomas Ogle, passed, in about 1817, to John Garth, who until 1809 had been the landlord of the Cheapside inn. At the end of 1819, his daughter Margaret, married Richard Dodgson, and there is documentary evidence showing that they were running the business from 1831. There are records of others managing the house in the 1820s, but there is nothing to indicate whether the Dodgson's had an involvement. John died in 1823 at the age of 63, and a property sale notice in the Preston Chronicle about ten years later in 1834, and instigated by his wife, Elizabeth, would indicate that the Garth's owned a huge amount of property, much of which surrounded the Garth's Arms.

By 1833, Margaret was to find herself widowed, but she continued to run the inn, named after her father, for a further four years, and, I suspect, it is likely to have taken a great deal of the next three years to complete all the sales of property, before she could live her life in a more comfortable manner.

A family ownership that extended to a period of forty-three years began in 1897, when the inn was bought by Levi Yates, described as a gentleman of St. Paul's Square. When he died in 1933 at the age of 83 years, his obituary contained details that you would think applied to somebody from an earlier period. He was described as 'one of Preston's best known sportsmen', but they were sports that many would associate with gambling. The coursing of dogs, and the trotting and racing of horses, together with the thrill of cock-fighting in his younger days. Cock-fighting was banned in this country fifteen years before his birth, but Scotland lagged behind by sixty years, so maybe it was there he went to enjoy his sport? Or maybe not?

In his younger days he was a champion shot before live pigeon shooting became illegal, but although the sport was largely abandoned before the turn of the century, it was 1921 before it was finally banned.

Levi Yates was said to be the 'father' of bowling in Preston, and took part in the Talbot Sweep in Blackpool.

The inn was run mainly by his son, Frederick, on two occasions, and between those two occasions by Levi himself. He took the licence at the age of sixty-three, and still held it at the time of his death in 1933. Frederick continued until 1940, but four years earlier, when King Edward VIII was obliged to abdicate the throne, a new role was found for him as the Duke of Windsor. Frederick Yates, it was said, was so upset at the abdication, that he changed the name of his house to the Duke of Windsor Inn. It continued in that name for about forty years.

Levi Yates junior, was a well-known building contractor in Preston, and I'm sure he has a story of his own.

The Inns of the Diarists

Possibly five-hundred years has passed since diaries first became fashionable. Not necessarily the diaries that are as well-known as those of John Wesley and Samuel Pepys, but more the day-to-day activities of individuals who were usually, but not necessarily, important members of society. They are, in themselves, pieces of local social history, and can be of great assistance to historians.

At the end of the 17th and beginning of the 18th century there happened to be a few such diaries kept, and Preston was a particular beneficiary of them. Unfortunately, since that time, nothing of significance has been repeated. Probably the most important of our diarists was Thomas Bellingham, who recorded his activities between 1688 and 1690. He was an officer in the army who was stationed in Preston during those years and moved about among many of the local gentry. His simple recording of his daily affairs rarely included other than his social activities, giving mention to those with whom he was mixing. They included the leading gentlefolk and their families, invariably consorting with them in the inns and taverns of the town and considering the small population of Preston at the time, there appear to have been a considerable number of them.

Bellingham also appears to have shown a deal of honesty in his records, for "was at ye ale house," and "drunk too much," were frequently used phrases.

Probably the two inns most frequently mentioned were the Ancor or Anchor, and the Mitre, but where were they? Anchor Weind was the narrow street that ran from the end of Lord Street and Back Lane through to Friargate and was the home to the thatched Virgins' Inn. It had been known by other names like Fryer's Weind but was renamed to take account of the fact that "the Anchor Inn stood directly across from the southern end of the passage", in

Anchor Court. Ancor, or Anker, were liquid measures used in Europe, and particularly in Holland, with whom there has been a long connection with Preston. The iconic timber-framed buildings by the old Town Hall and facing the Market Place were constructed by Dutch craftsmen. I have reason to believe that the same inn was at one point known as the Three Tuns, for in an account of the Market Place, written in the Preston Chronicle in 1855, it talked about the habit of men gathering around the Market Cross, "As was their custom in an afternoon, to gather and talk the politics of the day, and to quaff from the foaming jug, supplied from the neighbouring Three Tuns or Anchor". There have been Three Tuns in both High Street and North Road, but none that would fit the context of the article in question. Interestingly, a tun is a measure of liquid as well.

Examples of his diary entries for the Anchor we find, "Ye 9th May 1690 – Sir Edward Chisnell treated ye Mayor, Aldermen and Common Councell att ye Anchor," "Ye 3rd April 1689, Dean Pullein and Aldermen Singleton came hither – I sup't with them at ye Anchor and stayed till it was very late," and "16th August 1689 – was with Dr. Wroe at ye Anchor".

The last gentleman mentioned was the well-known 'Silver-tongued Wroe" who had preached the Guild sermon in 1682. Tobias Pullein (1648-1713) was the Yorkshire-born bishop of Dromore in Ireland, who had been obliged to flee to England as the Jacobites advanced towards his parish. He was welcomed into Preston by Thomas Bellingham and other sympathisers.

It is necessary, if not important, to maintain a distinction between the last inn and the Blue Anchor Inn which is of later provenance. It was situated in Blue Anchor Yard which, unlike its immediate neighbour, and running parallel to the north of it, did not extended as far as The Shambles. Its neighbour was The Strait Shambles, and it was by the covered entrance to this thoroughfare that the original Mitre Hotel stood, overlooking the Market Place.

You may see this passage erroneously referred to as Straight Shambles, and while its course takes no detours, the word 'strait' is descriptive of its narrowness.

Both our diarists spent time at the Mitre Inn, Market Place, where the landlord was Henry Turley. He was the landlord in 1684 when Kuerden described him on his hand-drawn map of that year, and he was certainly still present when mentioned by the diarists later in the decade. As was often the case, names were spelt phonetically, and in this case, as Tirlers and Tirlaghs:

Bellingham: February 2nd, 1689 - "First at Ratcliffe's then Tirlaghs."

Laurence Rawsthorne: May 14th, 1687 - "Tirlers and Will Atkinsons,"

and June 18th 1687 - "At Preston and Talbot, and White Bull and Tirlers."

A contemporary diarist, albeit slightly earlier, was a close friend of Bellingham, Colonel Lawrence Rawsthorne, who's diaries ran from 1683 until 1689. Again, the Anchor is the most frequently mentioned alehouse, and he tells us that Will Tomlinson was the landlord at the time. At the time, Rawsthorne was living at Hutton Hall, and was married, for the third time, to a daughter of John Fleetwood of Penwortham Hall. The following are some examples of entries in his diary:

"5th December 1683 – Swore Mr. Jonathan Seed, Under Sheriff, at the Anchor." 2nd February 1684 – At Ancor, held a Special Session there. Under Sheriff and Clerk o'th Peace with us and Jury." Other undated entries include: "At Ancor about affiliation of Alice Dymmock her bastard child," and "Dyned at Ancor and invited thither by the Bailiff."

The examples shown from both diaries give some indication of how important the Anchor Inn was, especially in the conduct of

137

the town's affairs, with business seemingly being conducted in a somewhat convivial atmosphere. Indeed, it can be inferred from many entries to what extent the inns and taverns entered the daily life of particularly, the local gentry.

Bellingham refers on several occasions to an inn called the Talbot, and commentators have assumed that it was the one that persisted until the early years of the 20th century in Chapel Yard off Friargate. There had previously been a Talbot Inn on Friargate Brow, but where it was situated is not known. At the time we are considering, there was an inn on Church Street directly across the road from Patten House, later the home of the Derby family, called the Talbot Dog. It was known colloquially as either the Talbot or the Dog, and I believe that the license for these premises was transferred to the Old Dog Inn, also on Church Street, that began its life around 1750. The landlord of the Talbot Dog in the late 1600s was William Adkinson, and I am inclined to believe that these were the premises to which Bellingham was alluding. His entry for 14th November 1689 read, "I was invited by several freindes and carried to ye ale house, and entertain'd by them. Mr. Birch was with us att ye Talbot." This is likely to be a reference to the Reverend Thomas Birch, Vicar of Preston at the time. He was said to be an unpopular character on account of his dull sermons. Earlier, on March 13th of the same year, both diarists recorded a similar message, with Bellingham writing, "Ye Dogg, with a friend from Ireland," and Rawsthorne recalling it as "Will Atkinson's with Bellingham and an Irish gent." Almost twelve months earlier, on the 29th of March 1688, he wrote, "At Preston and at prayers, and at Mr Lemon's to visit young Mr Blundell, and at Swansey's 'ith weend with Coz: Rishton of Antley, and brought him to Will Atkinsons, the Talbot."

An interesting entry in Bellingham's diary was where he recorded that he had been to visit Major Farrington, probably in Leyland. Henry and George Farrington were the sons of William

138

Farrington, who was already deceased, and although it is not certain which of the two sons he was referring to, it was Henry who was generally known as Major, and the place would be either Worden Hall or Worden Old Hall. He wrote, "went to see Major Farrington, who lies very ill of ye gout and stone. He told us he had beere of nine years old." It seems a strange juxtaposition of sentences. Was he telling us that the latter was thought to be the cause or the cure of the Major's illness?

Regular reference to the names of landlords and landladies of taverns and alehouses can be found in the diaries of both men, frustratingly omitting the name of the premises. For instance, Rawsthorne wrote on the 12th of June 1684, "At the Court of Election, was with Mr. Mayor, etc., at four tavernes and Margaret Wildings." A comparable entry in Bellingham's diary reads, "Att night took three cans at Rigbys, also drank three cans at Ratcliffs." It was after such nights he would record a confession such as "I was very ill all this day with last night's debauch."

In Lawrence Rawsthorne's diary, there is mention of The Boathouse, an inn on the southern, or Penwortham side of the River Ribble, close to the ferry, which will have been a convenient place for him to call on his journey from his home in Hutton into Preston, or on his way home. In his description of 17th-century Preston, Richard Kuerden suggests that the ferry was a quarter of a mile east from the bottom of Fishergate where there was 'the key or wharf over against the boat house, where diverse boats are ready, as occasion may require, for horse and foot to waft them over to the other side.' When Rawsthorne recorded a visit there on 21 November 1683 in his diary, it was already a hostelry, and its landlord was Edward Hollinhurst. Anthony Hewitson, the 19th century newspaper journalist, and owner of the Preston Chronicle, in his scrutiny of the diaries wrote as a comment, 'Edward Hollinhurst was or had been a farmer of the Preston Corporation Ribble Fishery,' but he gave no reference to validate the claim. He is buried in the graveyard of St. Mary's, Penwortham, and his tombstone reads, 'Here lieth the body of Edward Hollinhurst of Boat House who died the tenth and was buried the twelfth day of April 1686.'

A calculation from Kuerden's guide will put us in a position where the Bridge Inn used to stand, overlooking the river, on the corner of Leyland Road, and approximately the place where the 1759 bridge is now located. Rawsthorne often recorded that he met his wife there, as well as his brother-in-law Bro. Fleetwood.

The Boathouse became known as the Ferry Boat Inn, when in 1696 the former was demolished, with another building being erected on the same site by the Fleetwood's of Penwortham Hall. A stone seat, bearing the Fleetwood coat of arms, was built into the area over the entrance doorway. In 1826 the road to Leyland we now know, was diverted from the original Leyland Road to the ferry, only a short distance downstream, "and the licence was transferred from the Ferry Boat Inn to the present Bridge Inn." Interestingly, the stone slab bearing the Fleetwood coat of arms, was preserved by building it into one of the passage walls of the more modern houses erected on the site of the old building.

Left: The Ferry Boat and Old Penwortham Bridge, 1862

Photo: Robert Pateson

On December 15th, 1684, Rawsthorne recorded, "A hunting with Mr. Mayor about Midleforth (sic) and at the Boat House with him and Bro. Fleetwood after," and about five years later, Bellingham wrote, "Ye 24th June 1689 - very hott day. Dr. Leigh and I din'd at Penwortham. We had duck hunting in ye afternoon and call'd at ye Boat House." The River Ribble, apart from being known for the number and quality of its salmon, was also well-known for its ducks, particularly lower down the river towards Hutton and Longton.

Preston's geographical position at point on the River Ribble that is still affected by the tides, made it possible for vessels to bring goods into the town, even before the time when the river was dredged to allow larger boats access, the Boathouse and the Ferry Boat Inn, although only named for their place on the river, were in many ways the forerunners to those that followed and given more nautical names, almost all of which are close to the river or in the Marsh Lane area. The Old Quay Inn, which later became The Neptune, and its neighbour on the other corner of Marsh Lane, the New Quay Inn. In Marsh Lane we could find the Sailors' Home, known for a while as the Sailors' Return, the Mariners' Home, the Navigation Inn, the New Anchor Inn which, for a reason I've yet to discover, had previously been known as the Twin Sisters! Perhaps they were the joint landladies?

I have heard it suggested that the Jolly Tars Inn in Ladywell Street at its junction with Mount Pleasant was a nod to the sea, but I am more inclined to think that, as it was on the side of the new Lancaster and Kendal Canal, it was more of a jocular allusion to the Irish navvies who had constructed the canal and the bargemen who patronised the inn. It was they who hauled coal in a northern direction, before returning with limestone or marl on the return, and had previously been known as the Packet Boat Inn. The Lamb and Packet Hotel on Friargate was, despite having a large galleon on its inn sign, just another reference to the more mundane canal traffic.

The Lamb and Packet stood on the corner of Kendal Street, which had previously been known as Canal Street, a thoroughfare that ran from Friargate as far as the canal.

I have allowed myself to digress a little here, but I shall deal more fully with these connections and others at another time.

Returning to the story of the diarists and returning of the centre of Preston. A walk down Main Sprit Weind from Church Street or Fishergate, for this is the point where the two streets commence their outward journeys, is not one that anyone would deliberately make, unless they were visiting premises in the weind. There are not many of those left. Some eighty years ago it was described as a 'dismal, steep and uninviting passageway, overshadowed by large buildings on either side, and without interest,' and nothing has changed.

It is difficult to imagine that at the time of our diarists, it was a popular residential quarter of the town. On the east of the Weind, which is the left-hand side from Fishergate, close to the bottom, was where the old Coffee Gardens referred to in the Court Leet Records and were said to be famous in the annals of old Preston. In Rawsthorne's diary there are many entries noting his visits to Swansey's in the Weind, the name of the proprietor, and on two occasions, Bellingham mentions the same place.

I can only say that Swansey's was only thought to be an inn, or alternatively, a place of refreshment on this site. It had a bowling green attached where the diarists recorded playing. It was certainly a place of importance, particularly with the gentry, where Rawsthorne recorded that seventeen men dined there at one time, perhaps an indication that things other than liquid refreshments were available.

Following on the heels of our two diarists, were two more who occasionally visited Preston and made mention of inns. They were Thomas Tyldesley and the Reverend Peter Walkden, a Non-

Conformist minister, who was a resident during the time of his diaries of Chipping. To supplement his meagre stipend, he acted in a small way as a farmer, and brought his produce, mainly eggs, butter and barley to sell. His butter always went to Madam Sudell, a shopkeeper on Church Street close to where Avenham Street now stands. His diary is an accurate and honest record of all the events that occurred on his visits, his sales, and his purchases. A mention of his 'penny pot of ale' was noted, along with his 'quartern of tobacco at 3½d.' He had a particularly old-fashioned way of referring to, and about, his wife, as 'my love,' a practice that endeared him to many. A typical example from his diary read, "September 27th 1729, my love and I got ready for Proud Preston, and about ten o'clock we set forward and went to Preston and put in our mares at the Flying Horse and my love went to Madam Sudells' with butter and eggs......."

The Flying Horse was situated in or around Old Cock Yard, a passageway that was also known as the Flying Horse Backside. Several such passageways in Preston acquired the same appendage, such as Cockshott's Backside.

The diaries of Thomas Tyldesley on the other hand dealt more with the area north of Preston, where he had a home at Myerscough Lodge, as well as Fox Hall in Blackpool. His diaries tended to be a chronicle of his personal ailments, but it is thought that most of those could be laid at the door of his excessive drinking. He did occasionally visit Preston, where he would stay at the White Bull on Church Street, thought by some to be the origins of the Bull and Royal Hotel. He would there meet "his friend dear Nan Winckley" of Bannister Hall.

This chapter has been adapted from an article by J. H. Spencer, a reporter with the *Preston Herald* in the 1940s. Articles, records and resources relating to the history of Preston can be found on the wonderful website www.prestonhistory.com.

Where did that name come from?

Over fifty houses took their names from a specific trade. Occasionally, evidence comes to light that indicates that the name coincided with the occupation of the first landlord. Such was the case when we looked at the Spinners' Arms and the Spindlemakers' Arms, but it may also apply to many more, including:

The Coopers' Arms, Bridge Street. Often, the man of the house would continue with his trade whilst the tavern was run by his wife or other members of his family. The Coopers' Arms only existed in that name for the time of its occupancy by James Hall, the cooper. Whether it changed its name after he left, or whether it ceased to be a beerhouse, is not known, but there was no further record of it. Exactly the same can be said of the **Plasterers' Arms** in Glovers' Court. Joseph Billington was a plasterer by trade, and in 1834, his wife, Tabetha, was running the beerhouse.

The Anglers' Arms, on Avenham Lane only operated under that name from around 1865, and the landlord, Peter Longton's passion was as an angler. Angling Club dinners on the premises were held from 1871 to 1881, which, ironically was after Longton had left to take the **White Hart Inn** in Gin Bow Entry. The Anglers' Arms had previously been called **The Fat Scot(t),** which was the name of a breed of sheep, and a sheep market and abattoir stood right across the road from the pub**.** To add a little mystery, a field on which a part of the Avenham houses were built, was 'Scot's Field'; and to add a little interest, in 1855, Matthew Brown the brewer, was the owner of a Fat Scot of the pure Highland breed, which was slaughtered by Friargate butchers Smith and Yates. It was said to be on display in their shop window, and the fat alone weighed an incredible 200lbs. "On opening the beast, the man of steel dropped his whittle and stood astonished at the sight of the loins." A whittle is a knife, and a steel is an alternative name for a knife sharpener. Preston has also had a beerhouse called **The Whittle and Steel,** on Back Lane, now Market Street.

You will also recall that Matthew Brown called his first public house **The Anglers' Inn** (Page 31), this time a reference to his pastime.

The Amby Power beerhouse in Dale Street presents a mystery. The only certainty is that there is an Irish connection. The street, as well as the beerhouse, nestled under the northern wall of Horrockses Mill, built in 1791, opposite the prison, and was the final turning before Church Street was reached. A keen eye may still make out its position today. The Rev. Ambrose Power was an Irish Anglican Priest, whose Archdeaconry covered two sizeable Diocese, and he was therefore probably well-known to many of the mill workers and residents prior to their removal to the mainland.

Right: The Ambrose Power Memorial, erected in 1872, stands in The Square, Lismore.

It is worth noting that there was also an Irish entertainer called Amby Power. He was described as a delineator, or portrayer, of Irish life, and his use of a fiddle to accompany his performance gained him the name 'The Irish Paganini'. When the beerhouse first acquired its name in 1859, both men were well established in their respective careers, and for completely different reasons held a special place in the hearts of the local Hibernians.

In another part of the town, Canal Street, now Kendal Street and its environs, at the foot of Friargate, an area also populated by Irish immigrants and those of Irish descent, there could be seen a declaration of national identity in the naming of beer houses. **The Daniel O'Connell** on Pottery Hill, and the **Heart and Shamrock** in Back Canal Street were two of them. Friction with the non-Irish population was commonplace in this area and Friargate, so it is perhaps not surprising that the latter of these beer houses was once called **The Olive Branch.**

In 1870, **The North Lancashire Hotel** on Friargate Brow, fleetingly acquired the name **Prince Patrick Hotel,** when the licensee, Peter O'Malley, himself a thick-bearded Irishman, appeared before the magistrates charged with allowing six men to play dominoes on his premises. His father, Patrick O'Malley, a resident in the house, and quite likely one of the transgressing domino players, clearly had his name borrowed for the occasion in an attempt to protect the debatably good name of the North Lancashire Hotel.

The Royal George Inn, Hudson Street; **The Old Royal George** and the **New Royal George,** 154 and 170 North Road, respectively, were named in respect of a maritime tragedy.

Left: The loss of the 'Royal George' at Spithead, 1782.

Tragedies, such as the sinking of the Royal George, a 100-gun warship of the Royal Navy, off Portsmouth, were not uncommon in the naming of public houses, but odd that it should have happened so long after the event. The ship had been deliberately rolled to reveal parts of the hull that would normally be below the waterline, to allow repairs to be effected. However, the roll became unstable, water entered through the port holes, and in little time it sank. Eight hundred seamen lost their lives, including the captain, whose cabin door was forced shut by the pressure of water, and around two hundred others were saved.

The only explanation I can offer is that the ship had been launched in 1756, and 1856 would have been the centenary of that event. It was also the year that the Seven-Year War began, a war in which the Royal George figured prominently.

The Ocean Monarch beerhouse stood at the corner of Sydney Street East and Back Sydney Street, close to St. Thomas's Church on Lancaster Road. The first of those names was to differentiate it from Sydney Street, which was close to St. Peter's Church on Fylde Road.

Right: A burning Ocean Monarch in Liverpool Bay off the Great Orme, Llandudno.

The yacht, Queen of the South is in the foreground.

Painting by Harry Melling

The Ocean Monarch was a 1,300-ton American passenger liner, taking emigrants to a new life. Sadly, In August 1848, 178 of the 396 passengers got no further than Llandudno, their lives ending off its shores six miles distant. A cargo of Potteries area plates and other crockery, packed tightly in straw in the hull of the vessel, was probably of little assistance in a fire.

The beerhouse opened the following year.

Friendly Societies with the common aim of aiding the needy, often provided the name on the sign outside an inn. Some saw their name used more than once, and an indication of that number in Preston alone, is included after the name: **Druids' Arms,** (just one)**, Foresters' Arms,** (four times), **Oddfellows' Arms,** (9 times), **Free Gardeners' Arms,** (3 times)**.

In addition to those, individual lodges of each of those Societies would meet in the Club Rooms at inns and taverns which carried a different name on their sign board.

Names connected with sports often appeared as the name for an inn, with some less obvious than others, and others being used for a limited time only. An example of the first type was the **Hoop and Crown** on Friargate, an inn whose history stretched back to the 1700s. It had a short break during that century, when it was used just as a private residence, but resumed as a licensed house under the same name. The Royal Hippodrome was erected next door to it.

148

The name of the inn has its connections with the game of croquet and are parts of the same piece of equipment through which a ball is driven with a mallet, a long-handled instrument not unlike a short-handled wood-workers' tool. The hoop is made of metal and consists of two upright stems a maximum of 4 inches distant from one another, and the crown, at the top, around 12 inches from the ground, joining them together. The Hoop and Crown closed its doors just before the Second World War.

The perennially popular sport of bowls has been recognised in three **Bowling Green Inns.** One, in Edward Street, off Friargate, became the **North End Hotel** after Corporation Street had been created. The latter stood at the corner of Edward Street and the new thoroughfare, and although the idea is tempting, it has nothing to do with our football team, Preston North End. It was a reference to the nearby portion of the Lancaster Canal, with the final stretch of the waterway being known as the 'North End'. That was to distinguish it from the proposed 'South End' which it was to join on the other side of the River Ribble. However, the money to extend the canal ran out, and the Old Tram, or Owtram's Bridge was built instead, carrying the rail lines that ultimately connected the Lancaster Canal with the Leeds to Liverpool Canal. Owtram's were the company who constructed the bridge, and there is a school of thought that suggests that 'Old Tram' is merely a corruption of Owtram.

A second **Bowling Green Inn** appeared on the main Longridge road in Ribbleton, and a third was the replacement name for the **New Bridge Inn** by the side of the River Ribble and North Union railway bridge, details of which you will have seen in the chapter 'Down by the Riverside'.

Not far from the riverside, was the **Cricketers' Arms** South Meadow Lane.

It may not be a surprise to find that the family involved when the place first opened in 1864, were involved with cricket. The name was Coward, and brothers Cornelius and Frederick were professionals with both Lancashire County Cricket Club, and later Preston Cricket Club. The Preston club played their matches in the same place as they do now, on South Meadow Lane, with access also from West Cliff. On and off, various members of the family ran the inn over a period in excess of 25 years. In 1877, Cornelius (popularly known as Kerr Coward), became the landlord of **The Bowling Green Inn** on the Riverside at the end of South Meadow Lane, and remained there for four or five years. He also taught, presumably cricket, at Stoneyhurst College, and for many years umpired cricket matches at county and other levels.

On the other hand, the **Cricket Inn** stood in Alfred Street, off North Road. I have no explanation as to why or how it acquired its name. It may even have had the image of a grasshopper-like creature portrayed on its hanging sign, but that is only my own conjecture.

Examples of sporting names adopted for limited periods only were the **Cotherstone,** a name which interrupted the life of the **Star Inn** at the corner of Lawson Street and Walker Street. It happened when the former ostler at the Bull and Royal Hotel took over the

Star Inn in 1843, and renamed it after the horse, Cotherstone, which had won the Epsom Derby of that year.

A horse that was famous locally following an impressive series of wins in the annual Derby-family sponsored races on Moor Park and Fulwood Moor, was **Doctor Syntax.** It won its first race as a three-year-old in Preston in 1814, and between then and 1823 it won seven Gold Cups valued at £100 each in Preston, as well as ten similar prizes at Lancaster and elsewhere. Out of forty-nine races, he won on thirty-six occasions.

Preston had two taverns carrying the name of that horse, simultaneously for a short time around 1840. The first was in The Shambles in the town centre, with the other in Fylde Road. The latter building still exists but is now the home to a Chinese Restaurant.

Above: The Doctor Syntax

The Flying Dutchman was the name of an inn in Queen's Street, that took its name from the horse that had won the Epsom Derby in 1849, six years after **Cotherstone** had won the same race**.** He won all but one of the fifteen races in which he competed in a four-year career, and as well as the Derby, he won another of the Classics, the St. Leger. The name was adopted for the inn shortly after the Derby win, and retained it throughout its life.

Closer to home was **The Lady of the Lake** in Tithebarn Street. Not only was it the name of one of Scott's novels that had been performed at Preston's Theatre Royal more than once, but it was also the name of a horse that was owned locally and raced at many venues throughout Lancashire. At one time it was owned by

Robert Atkinson, the landlord of the **Sir Walter Scott Inn** at the corner of Lord's Walk and North Road. Atkinson later moved to the **Horse and Farrier** on Tithebarn Street and, as we discovered in an earlier chapter, changed the name of it to **The Lady of the Lake.** Some twelve years later its name was changed again to the Market **Hotel.** It stood immediately opposite the end of Lord Street and the **Waggon and Horses Inn** (later **The Tithebarn Hotel**).

Humphrey's Clock was a beer house tucked away in Addison's Yard, off Church Street. It was only a few steps from Main Sprit Weind which stands at the conjunction of Church Street and Fishergate. This beer house seems to have enjoyed a number of lives in different names, with some of the addresses given as Main Sprit Weind. They were premises that could be accessed from both alleyways. Master Humphrey's Clock was the name of a weekly magazine written and published entirely by Charles Dickens in 1840 and 1841, and although there is a suggestion that the beer house acquired the name prior to 1845, I only have evidence of it from that date. Dickens visited Preston in 1867, staying at the Bull and Royal Hotel, by which time the beer house had changed its name to **The Pilot,** and was being run by retired Preston Borough Police Sergeant James Palmer. At the same time, and only a few strides away across Main Sprit Weind, retired Preston Borough Police Inspector, Finlay Ringland, was for a short period, running the **Golden Ball Inn.**

The Robin Hood Inn and **The Little John Inn,** were a coordinated pairing, neighbouring each other at the opposite corners of a ginnel in Atkinson Street, off Lancaster Road, despite a disparity in their age. The Robin Hood had been operating from 1841, but it took him twenty-seven years to find Little John, which only made its appearance in 1868. Neither attracted a great deal of attention in their back-water positions, until as late as 1920, by which time the Robin Hood had closed its doors, and court proceedings against the landlord of the other one allowed a journalistic play on words to invent the eye-catching headline "Long Pull at the Little John". In an attempt to give good measures of beer to his customers, he overstepped the mark and fell afoul of the weights and measures inspector, who took a dim view of the practice. It was not an uncommon practice, and probably highly popular with the customers.

In the unlikely setting of Hope Street, off Friargate, there stood a beer house that enjoyed a number of names, from **Bretons' Arms** and **Britons' Arms**, to **British Arms** via **Whittle's Arms** and just the plain **Hope Street Tavern.** However, for two periods it was known as **The Paganini Tavern.** For the first time it was in recognition of the appearance of the Italian violinist and composer, Signor Nicolò Paganini who appeared at the Theatre Royal in Preston in 1833, before creating a sensation by eloping with the pianist's daughter. He succeeded in reaching the docks in London before being prevented from onward travel.

It made another appearance as **The Paganini Tavern** in 1853, by which time, as we discovered with the **Amby Power** beer house, Ireland had their own Irish Paganini, and Hope Street, a neighbour of Canal Street, was heavily populated with and frequented by, Irish folk.

The Judge and Struggle was a beer house on High Street, which also enjoyed access from Ormskirk Road. In fact, for most of its life it was known as **The Ormskirk Tavern.** The Struggle was a weekly newspaper published by temperance advocator Joseph Livesey, but it was more about the struggle against the Corn Laws and their abolition. The 'Judge' half of the name remains a mystery. It has been suggested that judges passed along High Street on their way to the Sessions courts in Lancaster, as well as on their return to their lodgings at the Bull and Royal Hotel, but I feel that idea is far too tenuous to be factual.

The Crystal Palace was a beer house in Hopwood Street, off Park Road, that memorialised the Great Exhibition of 1851 held in Hyde Park, London, in a temporary structure that was named, the Crystal Palace. It opened in 1853, the same year as the **Hyde Park Inn** on St. Paul's Road, possibly another reflection of the exhibition.

The Packet Boat Inn on Ladywell Street at its junction with Mount Pleasant West, and **The Lamb and Packet** at the foot of Friargate on the corner of Kendal Street, are two houses that share the word 'packet'. The former became the **Jolly Tars and Packet Boat Inn,** before dropping the second part to become, simply, **The Jolly Tars.** It stood apart from the Preston to Kendal Canal by the width of Ladywell Street, and it is an irony that the only navigators had been the navvies who had excavated and created a canal.

The name of the recently closed **The Lamb and Packet Hotel,** has been a source of contention over the years. It had been known by that name since it opened in 1807 but stood about twelve feet further forward into Friargate. However, in 1876 it was demolished and reconstructed in its present position, in order to widen the exit from Friargate at a time when Adelphi Street was opened up. At the Whitsuntide Festivities, immediately prior to demolition, the hotel was clearly patronised by the neighbours in Canal Street and its environs when William Richardson, the landlord, joined a procession with a banner displaying an Irish harp, with rose, shamrock and thistle, and the inscription 'Céad míle fáilte', literally one hundred thousand welcomes. Perhaps the thistle was included, because their next-door

154

neighbour in Canal Street was **The Sir William Wallace Inn,** and the rose for anybody English? In the picture, above, taken by Arthur Chappell, you can see one of the signs that has adorned the front of the Lamb and Packet Hotel over the years. The Lamb of Preston is easily explained, but the vessel on the board has never been seen on the canal, 300 metres distant along Canal Street, and I believe an ocean-going liner even made an appearance on the sign at one time, an even more incongruous image.

Battles, such as **Sebastapol Inn,** on Lark Hill Street, was named after the struggles at that place, and particularly wartime-leaders have figured prominently in names of taverns in Preston, including **General Havelock,** who probably took a dim view of the Plungington Road inn being named after him, because he was staunch teetotaller.

Above: The white-haired General Havelock casts a disapproving eye over those who enter the door beneath his vantage point. He died three years before the inn was named after him.

The **Duke of Wellington** had taverns named after him in Bedford Street and Tulketh Road, along with **The Wellington** in Glovers' Court. **The Waterloo Hotel** on Friargate, commemorates the battle where he conquered Napolean, but even the latter, who met his Waterloo in the June of 1815, got a mention by way of the **Napolean Inn** in Bushell Street, off Lancaster Road, but not until 1851.

A less obvious reference to Wellington was enjoyed by **The Hero of Vittoria,** which stood at the corner of North Road and Edgar Street, with its painted sign depicting Wellington with sword raised, mounted on a charger, and bearing the inscription 'The Hero of Vittoria'. Commanding the right wing of Wellington's army in this battle was General Lord Hill, who is remembered in the name of Hill Street off Friargate, and Hill Place, Fishergate, as well as **The Lord Hill Inn** on Adelphi Street.

Nelson was remembered in the **Lord Nelson Inn** on North Road, and the **Nelson's Monument** on Ribbleton Lane.

All of these, as well as many more, are important facts, but Preston had one beerhouse that was called **The Important Fact** in Ladyman Street. It was, for most of its life, known as **The Oddfellows' Tavern,** however,

In the Enumerator's Census of 1871 (above), when William Brown was the

Licensed Victualler, the place is described as the 'Important Fact,' at number one Ladyman Street, with the Kendal Castle next door at number two. It has to be remembered that in around 1910, number one was partially demolished to widen the street, and the Kendal Castle became the new premises on the corner.

Above: Later in the 1900's the wall to the left can be seen to have been breached to provide a side entrance into the wholesale fruit and vegetable market, now removed mainly to Fulwood. It was Good Street that Ladyman Street opened onto, with Good Street running off Bow Lane.

P**URE** S**PARKLING** A**LE,**

Splendid Home Brewed Porter and Bitter Ale, on Draught or in Bottle,

AT WILLIAM BROWN'S,

(late William Braithwaite's.)

EUSTON-STREET, OFF BOW-LANE.

The far-famed popularity of the

EUSTON-STREET BREWERY

is an

"I**MPORTANT** F**ACT**"

In the history of Preston.

Left: The use of the term 'Important Fact' seems to have been a marketing ploy, used by William Braithwaite and perpetuated by his successor. The Euston Street Brewery served several other inns in the town for a period.

Above: The day that every pub-goer wishes would arrive …… but it never does. This sign was seen in the Unicorn Hotel on North Road. I returned the following day to find that it had closed down!